WHAT WOULD
YOUR FATHER SAY?

Virginia Ruth Gunther

ALSO BY WINONA RUTH GUNTHER

PAPA SAID

Published by Inspiring Voices ©2012
Copies available from www.inspiringvoices.com, Amazon.com,
Barnes and Noble, and other bookstores

What Would Your Father Say?

WINONA RUTH GUNTHER

ISBN: 1499359225
ISBN 13: 9781499359220
Library of Congress Control Number: 2014908457
CreateSpace Independent Publishing Platform
North Charleston, South Carolina

Dedicated to all those brave men and women who have put their lives on hold while they served their country in the United States Armed Forces.

ACKNOWLEDGEMENTS

I would like to thank my wonderful daughter, Danna Gunther, and my dear niece, Christie Tam, for their combined efforts and many hours of proofreading and editing my book.

Many thanks to my dear grandson, Tim Gunther, for the many hours he spent preparing the photos for this book.

TABLE OF CONTENTS

PREFACE

At the urging of my family, I began writing my memories of the time I spent as a Hospital Corpsman in the Navy WAVES during World War II.

I was eighty-eight when I started this book. I am now 94. My memory is clear, but I am rapidly losing my eyesight. I have found, however, that one does not need eyes to see into their memories.

I close my eyes: It is early morning. The sun is just beginning to show itself as I stand on the steps of the WAVES quarters at Corona Naval Hospital with my friend, Vi. A soft morning mist wets our faces as we hurry up the hill to the Chow Hall and on to our assigned duties.

As I write of those wonderful men and women with whom I served, and the brave men I cared for on the wards, I can clearly see their faces and hear them speaking. It is as if we were together again, walking through the halls, wards, or offices at Corona Naval Hospital. We hurry down the steps to the Grand Ballroom. I hear the big band music and Joe Puccio singing as Herb meets me and we are dancing around the crowded room.

I see my little brother, Wayne, who entered the Service as a boy and came out a man, like so many of my patients. I hear their cries in the night and see the haunted look in the eyes of my patients as I listen to their stories of the horrors of the battlefield.

No one served their country in wartime without being affected in some way.

Regardless of whether you signed up before the war because there were no jobs to be had, because of a strong love of country, because you were drafted or signed up to beat the draft, or because you were looking for excitement, you bonded. Your Base became your home where you shared each other's joys and heartaches and grieved for those who were lost. People from all over the country, from different religious, cultural, economic and ethnic backgrounds, were thrown together and you broadened your thinking. You became a family, and outside that gate was a different world.

Clockwise from upper left: Raymond, Arthur, Mabel, Ruth, Wayne, Margaret, Josephine, Lois, Bob, Martha, Mary, Esther. Center: Dr. and Mrs. Hance Anderson

CHAPTER 1

Rumblings of War

"Papa, Miss Young asked the class to read the newspaper, pick out things going on in the world and write a paper explaining how these acts might affect us in the United States. Do you think Hitler will start a war that would ever involve us? Most of the class brings clippings about Hitler and what he is doing in Europe." The year was 1932, and I was in the sixth grade.

Papa looked over the top of his paper and said, "Yes, I do think we should be concerned about Hitler, but I feel we have more to fear from Japan. They have been buying up all of our scrap metal for years, building up their army, and they would like to have our natural resources. They are itching for a fight and now that they have invaded Manchuria, it looks like they are going to try to take over China a little at a time."

Since my Papa was the smartest man ever, I wrote my paper on Japan and proceeded to watch its progress on the world stage.

The years 1931 to 1941 began and ended with acts of violence by Japan. That decade was marked by the ruthless development of a determined policy of world domination on the part of Japan, Germany, and Italy.

In 1931, Japan seized Manchuria. Two years later, Germany withdrew from the Disarmament Conference and began rearming. In 1934, Japan gave notice of termination of the Washington Treaty for the Limitation of Naval Armament.

In 1935, Italy invaded Ethiopia. In 1936, Hitler tore up the Treaty of Locarno and fortified the demilitarized Rhineland Zone. In 1937, Japan again attacked China. In 1938, Hitler occupied Austria and dismembered Czechoslovakia. During the first half of 1939, Hitler completed the destruction of Czechoslovakia and seized Memel, while Italy invaded Albania.

In September 1939, Hitler struck at Poland, and during the two years that followed, almost all of the countries of Europe were plunged or dragged into war. In 1940, Japan entered French Indochina with threats of force.

Papa and I read the papers, listened to the news on the radio and discussed the events overseas and in Washington. One day he laid his paper aside and said, "I would rather be dead than see one of my sons go into combat." On May 30, 1941, my beloved Papa, at age 55, succumbed to a massive stroke. I was devastated.

There had never been such a funeral in Monticello. Papa's veterinary practice had taken him thirty miles in all directions, so everyone for miles around knew and loved Dr. Anderson. Grown men stood and wept openly at his casket.

Sprays of flowers covered six-foot-tall wire racks the full width of the church sanctuary. Those that wouldn't fit in the church were taken to the cemetery ahead of us and flowers were placed on every grave in the cemetery.

The church would not hold everyone, and in spite of the light rain that fell, the overflow crowd stood waiting outside on the sidewalk to follow the hearse ten miles into the country to our family cemetery. We passed farmers working in their fields. They stepped off their tractors, removed their hats, placed them over their hearts and stood at attention as we passed.

Grieving, I went back to work at White's Drug Store and continued to follow the war news on the radio, which was constantly turned to news when there wasn't a ballgame on. We knew the Japanese were talking to their counterparts in Washington, but the war in Europe was going so badly, everyone thought President Roosevelt would let us get pulled into it.

In late November, after emergency surgery, I decided to accept Betty and Leigh Stair's invitation to recuperate at their farm in Buck Creek, Indiana. I loved the farm, and Betty and Leigh were good friends and wonderful hosts. It was Sunday, December 7. I had been here two weeks and I had to go back to work on Tuesday.

We had finished lunch when Betty, seeing her sister-in-law in the yard, excused herself. "I'll be right back Ruth, I saw Leigh's sister at Mom Stair's. She promised me a recipe. I am going to run over and get it while she is there. I won't be a minute."

I turned the radio on to WGN and was listening to music. Picking up my book, I sat down to read. Suddenly, in the middle of a song, I heard,

> We interrupt this program to bring you a special news bulletin. President Roosevelt has just announced that the Japanese have attacked Pearl Harbor, Hawaii, by air. The attack also was made on all naval and military activity from the principal Island of Oahu.

I ran into the yard and shouted, "Betty! We are at war! Japan has bombed Pearl Harbor!" Betty and her sister-in-law came running. For the rest of the day, and all the next day, everyone was glued to the radio. We began to hear of the ships damaged and lost. The casualty list was growing. On Monday, December 8, at 12:30 p.m., President Roosevelt addressed a joint session of Congress and the nation via radio with his now famous speech, "A Day That Will Live in Infamy." The Senate responded with a unanimous vote in support of war; only Montana pacifist, Jeanette Rankin, dissented in the House. At 4:00 p.m. that same afternoon, President Roosevelt signed the declaration of war.

As I sat listening to the news of the terrible destruction, I remembered a conversation with my father in 1932, when he said, "Everyone is worried about Europe. It is true there is good reason for that, but I believe we need to worry more about Japan."

We all had friends in the military. During the depression, if their parents couldn't send them to college after graduating from high school, and since there were no jobs to be had, many young men joined the Navy, Army or Air Force.

The first thing I thought of was my brothers. Three were of military age. Raymond was married with one son. Arthur, who had recently married, was attending Texas A&M in veterinary medical school and planning to take over my father's veterinary practice when he graduated. Wayne was a senior in high school and had always been a daredevil. I was sure he would join after graduating.

I remembered Papa's statement shortly before he had his stroke. He saw no way we were going to be able to avoid war and believed Roosevelt was trying to get us into the war in Europe. I remembered him saying, "I would rather be dead than see one of my sons go into combat." Remembering that conversation, I thought to myself, God granted his wish.

On Tuesday, I returned to my job at White's Drug store in Monticello, Indiana. Mobilization of the country began immediately. We had declared war against Japan, and Germany lined up with Japan, declaring war on us.

Our country was not prepared for war on even one front. Now we had to fight on two fronts. The Draft was set up, and all men ages 18 to 64 were required to register. Young men were rushing to enlist. The radio in the drugstore played constantly, and townspeople gathered around it, anxiously listening for any news from the war front.

Patriotism was running high. Mothers with sons in the military were hanging flags in their windows. These were small white flags with a blue star in the center and a red, white and blue trim around the outside. One flag was hung for each member of the family serving their country. You could tell by walking down the street, which families had sons, daughters or husbands serving. If a Service member was killed, the flag was replaced with a white one with a gold star and gold trim.

Christmas decorations were put up, but it was not the season to be jolly. My hairdresser received word that her son, serving on the Arizona, had been lost. Two of my classmates, Jim Hoffman and Jack Condo, came home on leave for Christmas. They each came into the store to visit me before going back to base. They were serving in the Air Force at opposite ends of the country, training new pilots. The next day, someone came in and

5

said that Jack had been killed in a plane crash. Shortly thereafter, word came that Jim had been killed. He had crashed into a mountain in the west. Everyone thought it must be a mistake. How could two classmates, whom we had just seen, be killed in the same day at almost the same time at opposite ends of the country? Unfortunately, it was true. We had been at war for less than thirty days and already three gold stars hung in windows of three homes. War had dealt our little town of about 3500 people a terrible blow.

Jim's mother asked several of us who had graduated with Jim to act as flower girls at his funeral. When they played taps, there wasn't a dry eye among us. I had never attended a military funeral before and was not prepared for the loud bursts of gunfire as they fired over the grave. It certainly brought the war closer to home.

The following week, Mrs. Hoffman came into the drugstore to pick up pictures she had left to be printed. She looked through the pictures, turned, and walked over to me where I was stocking shelves. She held out a picture of Jim and asked, "Would you like to have this?" Tears welled up in my eyes as I thanked her. She put her arm around me, smiled, and left the store, a Gold Star Mother.

CHAPTER 2

How Can I Serve?

y brother Raymond, a contractor with a wife and young son, gave up his business and took a job with the Postal Service, working on the railroad. This was considered a Defense job: it meant he was away from his family three or four days at a time, but he didn't have to go into the Service.

Arthur was allowed to finish veterinary medical school at Texas A&M as long as he went 12 months a year and stayed in the ROTC until he graduated. He was considered in the Army to be a 2nd Lieutenant. On graduating, he would immediately report for duty.

Wayne was to graduate from high school in May. He would, no doubt, be the first of our family to serve.

It seemed our little town had suddenly been emptied of young men and women. Most of my friends had either gone into the Service or gone to a larger town to find wartime work. I was 22, working in a drugstore as an apprentice pharmacist and managing the soda fountain. I made the best sodas around, but I felt I had to do something for the war effort. I wanted to serve my country.

In February 1942, when I heard on the radio that the Army had formed the WACS and the Marines had formed the Women Marines, I went home and told my mother that I was going to enlist in the Marines.

Mom was shocked. "Why In the world would you want to do a thing like that? A daughter of mine in the Service! You can't be serious! What would your father say?"

I was ready for this response. "Mom, do you remember the picture in the parlor on the farm? It was a picture of a WWI soldier in uniform, leaning on his rifle, standing over his mother who was working in the field, harvesting wheat. The name of the picture was, 'A Son's farewell to his Mother.' I asked Papa about that picture, and when he explained it to me, I asked him if he had served. He said he had not, but would have been called in the next draft to serve in the Cavalry as a veterinarian; however, the war ended before he was called. I asked him if they allowed women to serve, and when he said no, I told him if they ever let women serve, I would go. His answer was, 'I would hope you would.' This is something I feel I have to do."

Mom looked at me for a long moment and asked, "When do you leave?"

"Tomorrow is my day off at the drugstore. I will leave on the morning train and come back the same day. Please don't mention this to anyone. I haven't told anyone of my plans and if I am turned down, I don't want to have to explain."

The following day, I took the train to Indianapolis and went to the Marine Recruiting Office. I spoke with a young Marine in charge of recruiting. He asked me several questions and told me the different fields of work in the Service. I could be in aviation mechanics, secretarial work, supplies, etc. I told him I wanted to be in the Hospital Corps. He explained to me that the Navy Corpsmen took care of the Marines. The Marines didn't have their own medics.

He tried to talk me into joining, but when I said I really wanted to serve in the Hospital Corps, he said, "I would love to have you enlist in the Marines, but if you want to care for the wounded, may I suggest that you wait a couple of months. They are forming a Women's Unit in the Navy. They should be enlisting in April or May." I thanked him and took the train home.

When I got home, I told Mom what had happened and that I was going to wait for the Navy to start enlisting women. I think she thought that was the end of it.

I went back to my job at the drugstore and waited. It seemed that every day, someone I knew received notice that their number had been picked or they would volunteer rather than wait to be called. I learned that my classmate, Betty Fisher, had become an Army Nurse.

Ruth at the drugstore

Everyone was doing what they could. It was amazing how fast our country was mobilizing. Volunteers acted as Block Wardens. Housewives saved every drop of grease for use by the government. Mom kept a coffee can on the back of the stove; when it was full of fat, she took it to Perkins Market. All the stores provided this service. Ration books were handed out. Of the many things that were rationed, those that seemed to be felt most were meat, sugar, and gas for cars. Few people complained. They felt they were doing something to help win the war. Mom used half as much sugar when she made her famous sugar cookies. She substituted honey for sugar in many recipes.

Everywhere you looked, on the movie screen and on huge billboards, you would see Uncle Sam pointing at you saying, "UNCLE SAM NEEDS YOU."

I began to see billboards and clips on the movie screen, asking women to join the WAVES and relieve a man for active duty.

The first week of May 1942, I boarded the train for Indianapolis to enlist in the WAVES. Reporting to the Enlistment Office, I was interviewed. I filled out the papers given me. One of the questions was, "Why do you want to join the WAVES?" That was easy: I wanted to serve my country. When I turned the papers in, I was sent to another room where I waited my turn for my physical.

The doctor to whom I was assigned was an old-time Naval officer, and his attitude left no doubt that he thought women had no place in the military. He could find nothing wrong with me physically, but when he checked my medical history and found that I had had surgery two or three months earlier, that was it. He told me the government couldn't take a chance on me because if I had complications, I might try to claim it was Service-related. I couldn't believe I had failed the physical. I was devastated. I couldn't hide my disappointment. The doctor softened slightly and said, "If you really want to serve, I would suggest that you go home and come back in one year. If you have had no problems in that year, you should be able to pass the physical."

Crushed, I went home and applied for wartime work with the War Manpower Commission. I was told that my work in the drugstore as an apprentice pharmacist was a wartime job and that I could not leave it for another job as long as I was needed there.

I continued working at the drugstore and listened to the news constantly. Lowell Thomas in Chicago came on every evening, telling us what was going on in the war. It seemed most of it was bad.

My brother Wayne graduated from high school in May of 1942. Many of his friends hurried to enlist as soon as they graduated. On December 21, although his number had not been called, Wayne and some of his friends took the train to Indianapolis and volunteered to be drafted. They were accepted and sent home to await orders.

On February 22, 1943, our family gathered at the depot to see Wayne off. I can still see him standing on the steps of the train. He looked so young. The light of the depot lit up his bright red hair. He was smiling that beautiful boyish smile of his and waving as the train pulled out. I stood behind the depot where I could watch, but no one could see me crying. To me he was still that little brother I had tried, often without success, to keep out of trouble. Wayne had always been a kid who took chances. I was afraid he would do the same in the Service.

Mom went home and hung a second Blue Star Flag in her window.

Wayne was sent to Fort Bragg, North Carolina, for basic training. He wrote saying he was assigned to the Glider Infantry. We had never heard of the Glider Infantry and thought he would have had to request that service, since pilots had to apply to get in. We were to learn that it wasn't a choice: it was an assignment you couldn't refuse. He added that he was the best shot in his company.

IS EXPERT GUNNER

Mrs. Gladys Anderson and family have received word that her son, Wayne Anderson, who is in army service at Camp Mackall, Hoffman North Carolina, had the highest score in his company of 164 men in a gunners test recently. He made a 98 score out of 100. An expert's rating is 90, and consequently the young man has been classed as an expert gunner.

Wayne sent greetings to all his friends here and said he is very grateful for the many letters he is receiving. He says he has been unable to answer them all as yet, but asks his friends to keep writing for letters are always very welcome.

Monticello Herald Journal

Wayne wrote to Raymond, saying he was going to be a machine gunner. That afternoon, I received a letter from him, saying, "This morning I wrote Red and said I was going to be a machine gunner. Since then I have changed my mind. I was talking to the Captain and he told me the average life of a machine gunner is one minute. I have decided to be a mortar man. They have another half minute". Wayne had not changed.

Early in May 1943, I returned to Indianapolis and reported to the Enlistment Office of the WAVES. Again I had to fill out papers before being sent for my physical. I had been assigned to the same doctor who had turned me down before. I thought he was going to deny me again because of a mashed fingernail, but he didn't. I was told to return home and await orders. I was so excited, I could hardly wait to get home to tell Mom that I had been accepted into the Navy. By this time, she had accepted the fact that I truly wanted to serve.

Two weeks later I received my orders to report to Chicago for duty. An officer would meet other WAVES and myself and escort us by train to New York. We were allowed to bring only one small suitcase. In New York we would be met and transported to Boot Camp at Hunter College in the Bronx.

Ruth Anderson Enlists in the WAVES

Miss Ruth Anderson has enlisted in the WAVES, and expects to be called within a month to take her basic training at Hunter College, New York. She has successfully passed all the necessary examinations following her enlistment in Indianapolis. She received her final physical examination in Chicago and took the oath of the WAVES in Chicago Friday. She will go to New York with a group from Chicago, taking her basic training as an apprentice seaman.

Miss Anderson was graduated from Monticello high school in 1938, and attended Oklahoma A. and M. college one year, taking a pre-medic course. She took a position at the White Pharmacy in June, 1939, and has been at the store since that time, continuing her position when the business became the Wynkoop Pharmacy. She will continue her work there this week.

Miss Anderson is the daughter of Mrs. Gladys Anderson and the late Dr. J. H. Anderson. She will be the third member of the Anderson family to enter the service of their country in the present war. A brother, Arthur, is a second lieutenant in the reserve at Texas A. and M. College where he is studying veterinary medicine. Another brother, Wayne, is in the glider infantry at Camp Mackall, Hoffman, North Carolina.

Monticello Herald Journal

I later learned that my sister Mabel had joined the Marines. Mom now had four Blue Star Flags in her window. Four of her twelve children were serving.

Mabel and Arthur in their uniforms

CHAPTER 3

Boot Camp

On June 2nd, 1943, Mom walked with me the two blocks from her home to the Monon Depot. We watched the train as it approached, belching steam and blowing its whistle. As it drew near, we could feel the sting of fine cinders being thrown up from the roadbed.

Mom stood silently beside me. Since she was not a person who showed emotion or handed out compliments, I wasn't sure how she felt about my going into the Service. The conductor took my suitcase, I gave Mom a hug, and she kissed my cheek as she returned the hug. I climbed the steps and turned to look back at Mom standing alone. Looking up at me she said, "Your father would be proud of you." I knew from that statement that she also was proud of me.

I chose a seat next to the window where I could see Mom still standing on the platform, smiling and waving as the train pulled away from the station. I felt sad for her, but excited for myself. I had no idea what the future held.

The train rumbled through town and into the country, picking up speed. Farmers were working their fields. Herds of cattle were grazing in the pastures. It was a beautiful day. The 100 miles from Monticello to Chicago seemed to take forever, but we finally pulled into the station.

A WAVE officer was standing on the platform, waiting to meet new recruits. I presented my orders and was told to join a group of other girls ready to board a train for New York.

The train must have been the first train on the railroad. It had hanging lanterns, and the springs in the seats were broken down. There were no Pullman cars, so we slept in our seats.

On June 4th, we arrived at Hunter College. I was assigned to a room with five other WAVES, Betty Keltner, Mary Jo Boadwin, Mary Chaney, Katherine (Kitty) Manion (niece of Senator Byrd), and Janette Green. Janette had posed for recruiting photos. She was a beautiful girl and as nice as she was pretty. They were a great bunch.

Circled: My five roommates and myself

We were informed that our luggage had been lost, so we would have to launder what we were wearing until it was found. We washed things out in the sink or tub and hung them to dry wherever we could find a spot not already taken. Sometimes our clothes were slightly damp when we put them on in the morning.

Uniforms were not issued for another week, but they issued our WAVE hats. Even with only our hats, children would run up to us and ask for our autographs. Every one was a patriot in those days. As I look back, I suspect that the lost luggage and lack of uniforms might have been deliberate to test us.

Hunter College had been taken over by the government for the WAVES. Like so many buildings during the depression, it had a lot of deferred maintenance. Plaster was coming off the wall in our room.

We were taught to make our beds the Navy way. There couldn't be a wrinkle. We had Captain's inspection every morning. One inspector gave our room a bad mark because of the falling plaster. We had twenty minutes to get up, make our bed, dress and report for muster on the parade grounds in front of the building. They lined us up and marched us to the Mess Hall.

After breakfast, we were marched to the Sick Bay for our required shots. We were then assigned to platoons, each with a Marine Drill Sergeant who was to teach us how to march. By the time we finished Boot Camp, we were good! We were marched to the Mess Hall, and before we were allowed to eat, every one was given a duty assignment.

I remembered people saying, "In the Service, you never volunteer." I forgot that advice when the Duty Officer asked, "Does anyone here know how to use a cash register?" My hand went up.

This was probably the smartest thing I did in the Navy. My duty was to run the cash register in the Officers' Mess. The others were assigned to the Mess Hall, Galley or the Scullery where they washed pots and pans. There was no air-conditioning in those days. They did have fans, but the temperature outside was a humid 90 to 106 degrees. The girls were passing out from the heat, or perhaps part of it was from the shots they had just received.

On Sunday, we were assembled on the parade grounds for church services.

Church service at Boot Camp

Aptitude tests were given and papers were filled out showing our education and work experience. We were instructed to look through the list of duties available to us: Hospital Corps, Yeoman, etc. We were told to list 1, 2, and 3, according to preference. After we made our three choices, we were given three locations in each category; we were to mark our location according to preference. Under the Hospital Corp, I could choose Florida, Chicago, or California. I had been to Chicago, and Florida was close enough to Indiana that I thought I could see it on my own someday. I reasoned that in my wildest dreams I would never see California, so that was my first choice, with Florida second. The officer in charge told us they would take into account our wishes, but could not guarantee that we would get what we chose. It depended on the need of the Navy.

We were taught a new language, the Navy Language. Ceilings were overheads, floors were decks, walls were bulkheads, the bath was the Head, the kitchen the Galley and the dining room the Mess Hall. The hardest thing for me to get used to was Navy time. One o'clock in the morning was 0100. One in the afternoon was 1300.

We were kept busy in classes, marching, exercising and working our duty stations from 6 a.m. to 7 p.m. Marine Drill Sergeants were in charge of our physical training and exercise. When they finished with us, we made them proud on the parade grounds. We were good.

Parade Grounds and close-up of Ruth's platoon marching on Parade grounds

Few of the girls washed out. Scuttlebutt had it that one girl broke under the pressure, slipped out and jumped off the Brooklyn bridge. If this rumor was true, none of us knew who she was and it was never confirmed.

When our uniforms finally arrived, we were marched to a large building, lined up and told to file past an officer who was telling us what size uniform we should ask for. She looked at me and said, "Size 14." I protested that I wore a size 12. She snapped at me and said, "I said 14." I moved on and asked the civilian handing out the summer cotton uniforms for a 14. Going into a fitting room, I tried it on, and went to the next booth to be fitted. Naturally, mine was way too big and the lady told me it had to be altered. I wasn't allowed to try a smaller size. I left the uniform to be altered, at my expense, and moved on for my wool Dress Blues, raincoat, and summer seersuckers. When the lady asked for the size, I said 12. They fit perfectly. I think someone was making a little extra money on alterations. We were then given heavy, black-laced "sensible shoes". I wore blisters on blisters with all the marching in those heavy sensible shoes.

After five weeks in Boot Camp, we received our orders. I was ecstatic. Not only did I get into the Hospital Corps, but was assigned to the Navy Hospital in San Diego for Corps School. Those going to Corps School were given little Red Crosses to sew onto our uniform sleeves. We were Apprentice Seamen.

We were given a one-day pass to see New York City. My roommates and I caught a streetcar and went into the city. We went to St. Patrick's Cathedral and attended Mass with one of the girls. We saw the Empire State Building, but no one was allowed to go up to the top because of security. This was also true of the Statue of Liberty. The boat to the island where the statue stood wasn't even running. One day didn't give us much time to see the city; nevertheless, we were thrilled to have been in New York City and to have seen it and the Atlantic Ocean.

Returning to our Barracks, we prepared to ship out the next morning.

CHAPTER 4

The Troop Train

We boarded the train in New York, but because of security we weren't told what route we would be taking or when we would arrive in California. "LOOSE LIPS SINK SHIPS."

Troop Train

The train was another relic they must have salvaged from the railroad junkyard. The seats had long since lost any cushion they might have had. They were lined up against one wall of the train, facing each other. Each seat held three passengers. At night these seats were made into six miserable bunk beds. Along the other wall was a narrow walkway. There was no air-conditioning in those days, so the windows were all open, allowing the hot air, along with dust and cinders, to blow through the cars.

After leaving New York City, we were told to look to the right and we would see West Point from our window. What a beautiful sight. After that, we didn't know where we were until we stopped in a station. At night, until lights were turned off, all curtains had to be drawn. Troop trains could be targets. This not only blocked the light, but the much needed air. We passed many troop trains with young soldiers no doubt heading for the East Coast to ship out to the European Theater.

It took us six days to cross the country. I don't know if it took longer because they sometimes pulled off to allow other troop trains to pass or if they took a roundabout way for security.

After we crossed the Mississippi, we went to the dining car only for breakfast. For lunch and dinner, we stopped at Harvey Houses all across the country. It was the same menu at every Harvey House: boiled beef and potatoes for lunch and dinner every day. The first couple stops, we enjoyed the food, but we were glad to run out of Harvey Houses.

Harvey House Restaurant

The train trip was exciting to me. I had never been more than 100 miles from my Indiana home, other than one year at college in Oklahoma. I had never seen mountains. I stood with other WAVES on the platform of the caboose while traveling through the Rocky Mountains. I could not get over their beauty. A train workman was sitting on the platform, playing his guitar, singing cowboy music and spinning wild tales of his life on the range. He probably had never ridden a horse, but we enjoyed the music. He actually had a very good voice.

The scenery changed drastically when we left the mountains and found ourselves in the desert. We saw Indians in their colorful clothes, tending their sheep or lounging in the shade in front of their hogans. There was sand as far as you could see.

Of all places, this is where our train broke down. With no air moving through the cars, they became like an oven. Our WAVE officer ordered us all off the train in full uniform: coats, hats, purses and gloves. She marched us up and down a dirt road in the middle of the day. It must have been between 110 to 120 degrees. The Indians sat around or stood in any shade they could find and watched us crazy white women. It is a wonder someone didn't have a heat stroke.

When they finally were able to get the train repaired, we boarded and stood by windows to catch the hot, dusty air. At least it was moving and, as hot as it was, it felt cool.

Our train stopped in the little towns of Santa Fe and Albuquerque, New Mexico. We saw the Navajo ladies in their colorful dress, sitting in any shade they could find, selling their jewelry.

Finally we left the desert and started climbing up the mountain to the town of Flagstaff, Arizona. The higher we climbed, the cooler the air became. It felt wonderful blowing through the cars, bringing with it the fragrance of pine from the wooded hillsides. For the first time in days, we slept well under a light blanket.

This cool air was welcome, but it didn't last long. We dropped back down into the California desert. Our train stopped in Needles, California, where we were allowed to get off the train so we could get some exercise.

The temperature must have been over 120 degrees. There were soldiers everywhere, getting water and resting. They came up to talk with us, telling us they had been here for weeks on desert maneuvers, preparing to join General Patton's army in Africa. Their faces were terribly sunburned, blistered and peeling, many with lips scabbed over from blisters that had burst. I felt sorry for them.

For years I had heard of the beauty of California. I kept watching for the flowers, but saw nothing but sand and rocky hills. When we pulled into San Diego, we were met by a Navy bus that was to take us to our quarters. I was thrilled to finally see San Diego.

Pulling out of the depot, we traveled through the business district to the Naval Hospital gates. Marine guards were manning the gates. The driver showed his I.D. card; one of the guards stepped in, looked around, stepped out, and waved us through. On top of the hill, we could see the hospital with its red tile roofs. I was finally seeing "Beautiful California." The Hospital grounds looked like a perfectly landscaped park. There were flowers everywhere. I wondered how they kept it so manicured and who mowed that huge lawn. This would be our home for six weeks of Corps School.

CHAPTER 5

Corps School

U.S. Naval Hospital, Balboa Park, San Diego, California

*A*fter passing through the gate, our bus traveled up the hill and stopped in front of a large barracks building where we were assigned quarters and were given our orders.

WAVES were told they were not allowed to stand around on the grounds and talk to the men. If we walked across the compound with a man, we were to walk at a "businesslike gait." If we returned from liberty after dark, we must be escorted from the gate to our barracks by one of the Marine Guards.

There was a ward of mental patients on the base. If a patient escaped, they blew a siren. If we heard the siren, we were to take cover immediately. It never blew while I was there. Scuttlebutt had it that an escaped patient had killed a nurse in Balboa Park a short time earlier.

Five days a week we attended classes for half a day; the other half we spent on the wards, taking care of patients. We learned about nursing in class and did it on the wards.

We had to learn to give shots, how to treat the wounded, and what to do in case of emergencies. We had to learn all the arteries, bones and muscles of the body. In addition to this training, we were instructed on what we were and were not allowed to do. We could not refuse to treat a Service man or woman, regardless of where we were or what branch of the Service or what country they were from. We had some Canadians training here.

Treating a civilian was a Court Marshal Offense (the one rule I broke later), because if anything went wrong, they could sue the government. They gave us the Navy Blue Book, and we were expected to read and understand its contents. All the Navy rules were in that little blue book.

We had to learn to identify all planes and ships, ours and the enemy's. The West Coast was always on the alert in case of attack from Japan. When not in class, we worked on the wards taking care of patients. This was on-the-job training.

The San Diego Zoo in Balboa Park had been taken over by the government, and the animals moved to other zoos. The buildings had been cleaned out and were used to admit patients before assigning them to wards. When a shipload of patients arrived, Corpsmen were bussed down to the park to take information from the patients and assign them to wards.

Our first group was from Guadalcanal. Their eyes showed the horrors they had been through. Nearly all of them had malaria. Many had casts, but all were ambulatory. The more severely injured patients had been taken directly to the Hospital. One Marine said, as I was checking him in, "Would you talk to me? It has been so long since I have heard an American woman speak." Some of them held back and seemed almost afraid of us.

Musicians and actors volunteered to entertain the patients. I wheeled one of my patients out onto the patio to hear the world famous violinist, Jascha Heifetz. He stood on a balcony above us and played. It was wonderful.

Ruth with patient

We had only been at SDNH for three weeks and were not eligible for liberty, when orders came out that any WAVE wanting to go to the Grant Hotel to dance with the Marines in the Grand Ballroom could have liberty. I think almost everyone went.

The bus met us at the gate and took us to the hotel. We walked into the ballroom and saw that most of the Marines were either drunk or well on their way. Edie and I, along with many of the others, walked in the front door and out the back. This gave us a chance to see San Diego before the bus came to pick us up.

My worst experience was gas-mask training. Gas masks were handed out and we were instructed on how to use them. We were then told to enter a Quonset hut, carrying our masks. When we were all in the hut, tear gas was shot into the building and we heard the order "Don your masks." I am apparently allergic to tear gas. When I came out, my skin was beet-red, my eyes bloodshot and tearing. I was this way the rest of the day. We had to go back on the ward and my patients were more worried about me than their own broken bodies.

We had been at USNH for four weeks when we were granted liberty for one day. Edie and I took the bus from the gate to San Diego. The first thing we did was look for a good place to eat. We didn't know that no restaurants were open in San Diego on Sunday. In fact there wasn't much to do. We decided to go up the outside elevator in the beautiful El Cortez Hotel. As the elevator rose, you could see the whole city and the camouflaged port. We walked back to base for dinner. You really couldn't beat Navy Hospital chow.

After 5 weeks of school and training, we were given tests that would determine our rate when we left Corps School. When our orders came, I learned that I was one of a few who had been advanced to the rate of Pharmacist Mate Third Class. Most of them were raised to Seaman First Class. I did study hard for the tests, but I think one of the reasons for my step-up in rate was my year of pre-med in college and the three years I had as an apprentice pharmacist. We were issued patches to sew onto our sleeves and told we would be receiving orders soon.

Advancement in rating to PhM3c

When we mustered outside the Barracks Saturday morning, we were met by a WAVE officer. She accompanied us to the Santa Fe Depot where we boarded a train for Los Angeles.

As we left San Diego, we traveled under camouflage that had been erected over streets and all buildings that had anything to do with military or the manufacturing of war-related products, which was most of San Diego. Looking up, you could see a screen that had been painted to look like tops of trees. This was true all along the West Coast wherever there was shipping or manufacturing.

The officer who met us in L.A. gave us a two-day pass and a list of places where service Women could find housing and entertainment. We were ordered to report back at a set time Monday morning.

Edie Gilbert

Edie Gilbert, originally from Findley Ohio, and I, had worked together in Corps school and had become friends. We headed for the Studio Club Guest House in Hollywood. This place was on the list we had been given.

We were given the address of a home in Hollywood, the owner of which had offered free lodging to Service women. They also gave us maps of Hollywood and tickets to a radio show called Command Performance. These shows were being broadcast only to our troops overseas. Only Service people could get these tickets.

After getting settled in a nice home near Sunset and Vine, we headed out to see Hollywood. I was disappointed in Hollywood. I thought it would be more like a movie set, and it was just a little town. We walked all over town, seeing as much as our two days would allow. We saw the actors' handprints in the sidewalk, the Brown Derby, and the Hollywood Canteen.

We tried to get into the Hollywood Canteen, but were turned away by the little starlet at the door. She said we could go up in the balcony and watch, but only Service <u>men</u> were allowed on the dance floor. We were furious, and as we stood there fuming and trying to decide where to go, a lady came out of the Canteen and asked if we would come in for a photo of Service people in the Canteen.

I said, "We just tried to go in and were told Service women weren't welcome."

"Well, this is just for a photo for the newsreels".

I politely told her where to put the Canteen. We were told later that the only women allowed in to dance were Hollywood starlets who did it for publicity, and they didn't want competition.

The radio shows we saw were wonderful. Bob Hope and Frank Sinatra put on one of the shows. You could tell they hadn't read the script before the performance, because they got so tickled at times they nearly flubbed their lines.

Our two days passed quickly. Early Monday morning, we reported to the Depot as ordered. The WAVE officer waiting for us gave us our orders. We were being sent to Corona Naval Hospital in Norco, approximately six miles North of Corona, California.

CHAPTER 6

Corona Naval Hospital

We boarded the train in Los Angeles and headed east to Riverside. After traveling through miles of vineyards, citrus groves, and small towns, we pulled into Riverside. I was struck by its beauty. A bus picked us up at the station and we traveled back west through the city. Beautiful, well-maintained old homes were nestled into acres of orange and lemon groves covering the hillsides. Well-kept smaller homes lined the streets.

When we finally reached the Hospital, the bus stopped at the gate. A guard spoke to the driver, glanced into the bus, and waved us on. Driving through the gate and up the hill, the bus stopped in front of a beautiful, Spanish-style building. This was the WAVE Quarters. We were ushered in and told we could choose any room not occupied.

WAVE Quarters, Corona Naval Hospital

The Hospital had not been open long. There were only thirteen WAVES on the base when we arrived. Edith Gilbert and I chose a room on the first floor. There were twin beds, two dressers and two chairs in the room. We had to go down the hall for the bathroom, but this was luxurious living compared to the Barracks where we had lived in San Diego. Several months later, we moved upstairs into a three-bed room with an adjoining bath which opened into the next room with two beds.

Corona Naval Hospital

Before the war, these grounds had been the Norconian Country Club, a very exclusive club that catered to the wealthy Hollywood crowd. The government took it over, as they did many properties throughout the country, for government use. I was told they paid market value for the properties they took. I learned later that the owners had never been paid. They were fighting in court over the amount the government offered. It was a beautiful property in the middle of nowhere. Perhaps this was one of the reasons it had been chosen.

Once we deposited our luggage, we were ordered back to the lobby for instructions, given a map of the base, and told to feel free to wander anyplace on the base in our free time. We could check out boats if we wanted to go rowing on the lake, and could even check out fishing tackle. There was a bowling alley at our disposal, as well as two Olympic-size swimming pools for use by patients and staff. A store and Ship's Service were located on the first floor of the Hospital. In the valley below the main Hospital was a beautiful chapel for Protestants. Catholics had their services in another location.

There were four Units on the base. Unit One was the main hospital, Unit Two for tuberculosis patients, Unit Three for rheumatic fever patients, Unit Four for wounded officers.

The base Fire Station and garage were next to our barracks. All enlisted personnel were required to have firefighter training. Between Riverside and Los Angeles, there were hundreds of acres of vineyards. When the Santa Ana winds blew in from the desert, all liberty would be canceled and we were to be available to fight fires. If a fire got into the vineyards, it could sweep all the way to Los Angeles. Those fire hoses were heavy. We got the training, but fortunately, I never had to use it. If it was our liberty weekend and there was a suggestion of a Santa Ana, we got off the base as early as possible.

After getting settled, we were mustered out in front of the building and marched up the hill, shown through the hospital, and assigned to wards or special departments. Edie and I were assigned to different wards. We met again at the Chow Hall for lunch and dinner.

Every weekend, in the Grand Ballroom, there was a Ship's Dance. The hospital provided a live big band that played wonderful dance music until midnight. One of the Corpsmen, Joe Puccio, sang with the band every weekend he was on base. He had a beautiful baritone voice and had sung in his family's nightclub in Michigan. But for the war, he could have sung professionally. The band loved to have him join them on stage and he loved to sing.

WAVES were encouraged to attend the dances. It gave the patients, who weren't able to go on liberty, a little social life and someone to dance with. When we attended, we never sat out a dance. Patients appreciated it; even those in casts tried to dance, and we never turned them down. It was also a great way for us to make friends with the other Corpsmen.

Corpsmen worked 8 hours one day and 16 the next, with port-and-starboard liberty (which was liberty after work on our short days, with every other weekend off). It didn't take long to make friends with our fellow workers. It was like a big family. If we weren't dating someone, we went out as a group. We found the best eating spots around. My favorite was the Chicken Shack near Riverside.

In summer, because of the heat, our Dress Code was liberalized. With our summer seersucker uniforms, we were allowed to wear white bobby sox on base. If we went off base, we must wear hose. It was impossible to buy nylon or silk hose anymore. Nylon and silk had been reserved for military use.

I had some nylons that I had been so careful with, if I got a run in them, I would take them to a lady who could repair the run and you couldn't see where it had been. On our first liberty, I took my hose out of the drawer and found they were all full of runs, beyond repair. No one had told me that ants eat nylon. The girls who had been there for a while told us to keep our hose in glass jars. It was good advice too late for my nylons, but I kept my rayons, a very poor substitute for silk or nylon, in jars.

CHAPTER 7

My First Duty Assignment

There were two or three Corpsmen and one, sometimes two, nurses for a 20-to-30-bed ward of ambulatory patients. The Corpsmen took turns going to lunch.

The government uses first names. My full name was Winona Ruth Anderson. I had always gone by my middle name, but officially I was Winona. I don't know if they couldn't remember Winona or if they felt it didn't fit me, but within a short time the Corpsmen were calling me Andy. Soon my friends and the patients all called me Andy.

Almost all of the patients on my ward had malaria and Jungle Rot in varying degrees. Jungle Rot was thought to be an infection caused from not being able to keep your feet clean and dry, which was impossible for those wading through the swampy jungle. Some of the patients thought they had gotten it from scraping their feet on the coral when they swam in the ocean. It is similar to athlete's foot, only worse. I had cases so bad, they looked as if their feet had been scalded and peeled. We soaked them in pans of Permanganate of Potash solution.

My first day on the ward, a plane flew over the hospital. Several patients dived under beds. No one seemed to notice. They all understood.

Most of our patients were Marines. Many were on crutches, some in wheelchairs. The majority of them were from Guadalcanal. They said they landed on the Island to secure it and were supposed to be relieved by the Army in six weeks. The relief didn't come for six months. Supplies were stretched as much as possible, but they ended up surviving on whatever they could find. They told of eating wormy rice and scavenging for food from the packs of dead Japanese. One man said he lost his stripes for stealing food from the Officers' Mess.

These Marines were very bitter that they nearly starved on Guadalcanal, and yet, as they neared the California coast, they saw sailors throwing all unused meat and other perishables overboard before they reached port. This was ordered by the ship's officers because they knew if they came into port with leftover food, the government would figure they didn't need that much and would short their inventory on their next deployment. What a waste of good food!

The men were eager to talk of their experiences. One of the Corpsmen told me that the Japanese had learned to recognize the insignias on their uniforms and targeted Corpsmen. They reasoned that if they could take out the Medics, casualties would more than double.

Navy Corpsmen who were assigned to the Marines wore Marine uniforms with their Corpsman's Insignia on their sleeve. The first causalities off the landing craft were Corpsmen. When they realized this, they removed the Red Cross from their sleeve.

Corpsmen weren't supposed to carry guns, but they learned quickly that they were targets. They picked up guns that had been dropped by dying Marines and kept them close by.

The Marines didn't like the Navy, but they didn't consider their Corpsmen to be Navy. A Corpsman could mean the difference between life and death. The Marines knew this and would lay down their lives to protect a Corpsman.

If a Marine was wounded, he shouted "Doc!" and a Corpsman would respond. The Japanese picked this up and would call, "Doc!" from the jungle. When a Corpsman dashed out, thinking it was a wounded Marine calling, he would be killed or captured and tortured close enough so the Marines could hear his screams. The Marines showed me pictures and told me stories of how they retaliated. You wouldn't want to hear those stories.

Many told of miracles. One Marine told of being up in a plane when it was hit. He knew he was miles out at sea and nothing could save him. He knew he was going to die. Those were his last thoughts as the plane dove into the ocean. He awakened on the beach. Both of his legs were broken. No one else in the plane survived. He had no idea how he got to the island. Some speculated that dolphins might have brought him in. He didn't know how he got there, but he was sure God deserved the credit. Friendly natives found him and took care of him, hiding him from the Japanese until a rescue crew found him.

We cared for sailors who had been wounded transporting Marines in landing craft. Others had been rescued from ships that had been bombed or torpedoed. They told of the horror of seeing their shipmates, consumed in flames, jumping overboard to try to save themselves. They told of fighting the fires onboard ship until they were forced to jump into the water, praying for a rescue ship.

Those who were burned and jumped into the salty ocean healed better than those who didn't. The doctors believed the salt water kept them from losing body fluid. We were taught, in case of an emergency, to soak a sheet in saltwater and wrap a burn patient in it until he could be transported to a hospital. This knowledge came in handy later.

The doctors made morning sick-call every day and left orders for treatment if needed. Some patients needed surgery. The day before they were scheduled for surgery, it was the Corpsman's responsibility to tell them the time their surgery was scheduled and ask if they would like to meet with a Chaplain. If so, we would make appointments for them.

One Marine was scheduled for hernia surgery. When I asked him if he wanted a Chaplain, he cursed and said, "No! I don't believe in that stuff. I have never prayed in my life."

I was surprised by his outburst. All my other patients had wanted to meet with a Chaplain.

"You have never prayed?" I asked. "Not even the Lord's Prayer?"

"No I have never prayed. I don't even know the Lord's Prayer and I don't want to. There is something I want you to do for me, though: They tell me that when you are coming out from under the anesthetic, you say some pretty wild things. I am worried about what I might say. Promise me you will tell me what I say?"

I assured him I would be there to special him when he came out and would tell him what he said.

The next day, when he was brought back from surgery, I was there. The nurse set up his IV and left me to watch him. I wondered what he was afraid he would say and if I would want to repeat it.

When the anesthesia began to wear off, he started talking. He was saying the Lord's Prayer over and over. When he came to, the first thing he asked me was, "Did I talk? What did I say?'

"Yes, you talked, but you wont believe me if I tell you what you said."

"What was it I said? You promised you would tell me."

"Okay, but you didn't tell me the truth before you went into surgery. You said you didn't know the Lord's Prayer. You were saying it over and over again as you came out from under the anesthetic. If you didn't learn it from your mother or dad, you no doubt heard it many times on the battlefield. You didn't miss a line." He didn't believe me.

CHAPTER 8

Life Off the Base

*W*e had checked with the girls who had been here for awhile regarding places to go on liberty nights. They told us there was a bus to Corona, a small town about six miles from the hospital, but there was nothing to do there unless you wanted to hang around bars. They recommended the Mission Inn in Riverside.

Riverside was 12 miles from the hospital, and there was no transportation. This was our liberty town???? The Navy finds a way: You walk (out of the question after an eight-hour shift) or hitch a ride. What would Mom think? She wouldn't believe it, so why tell her.

On our first night of liberty, a group of us changed into our Blues and walked down to the gate. We caught rides with some of the civilian workers into Riverside. Edie had been told there was a ballroom in the Mission Inn, where they had a great band. She was right; we walked in and found a live band playing and several Corpsmen from the hospital standing around. When they spotted us, they rushed over and asked us to dance. We danced all evening and left together, hoping to find rides back to the base.

It was a breeze. No one going our way would pass up Service people. We felt safe with a Navy escort.

After that, we spent our liberty evenings in Riverside, dancing at the Mission Inn or finding good places to eat.

Being in the Navy was like being in a big family. We made it a practice not to date our patients, but there were a lot of lonely Corpsmen on the base, so we never lacked escorts. We always felt safe and protected with them. I tried never to get too attached to any of my boyfriends. The problem was, you would be dating a great guy for several weeks and he would get orders to ship out. You would hear from him for a while and then suddenly the letters would stop. Was he wounded or killed in action? There was no way of knowing.

One night, in Riverside, three of my WAVE friends and our dates had been dancing and were heading home when an MP stepped out of an alley and pulled my date aside, whispering something to him. He turned to me and said, "Stay here. I will be right back. Someone has been injured." As we waited, we heard sirens and saw the Navy ambulance pull into the alley.

When my friend returned, he said Zoot Suiters had attacked some Marines. One of them had been slashed across the abdomen. He was holding his own intestines in. My date had no way to help him other than tell him not to move until the ambulance arrived.

This was the era of the Zoot Suiters. These were Mexican gangs dressed in black: long coats with wide lapels and wide padded shoulders; high-waisted, wide-legged, tight-cuffed, pegged trousers with long heavy watch or key chains dragging from the belt to the knee or below, then back to a side pocket. They used these chains and knives in fighting. They originated in L.A. where there were riots between them, Sailors, and Marines. They had begun to show up in Riverside.

Most weekend Liberties were spent in Los Angeles. There were two department stores in L.A. authorized to sell WAVE uniforms. We could stock up on needed clothing while there. Our initial uniforms had been issued at Boot Camp, but after that, we had to buy our own. A uniform could cost half a month's pay.

After one of our shopping trips, we stopped in a restaurant for a quick lunch. When the waitress brought it, I noticed the pat of butter looked as if it had been dropped on the floor. I pointed this out to the waitress and she took it back to the kitchen. After a while she returned with the same pat of dirty butter. I looked at the butter and then at the waitress and said, "This is the same pat of butter I sent back."

She glared at me and said, "Don't you know there is a war on?" and turned away. Maybe she didn't notice we were all in uniform???

This attitude was not unusual when dealing with civilian women. Civilians usually ignored us. I tried to justify it by thinking of the sacrifices civilians were making that didn't touch Service people stationed in the States. We ate well, not even thinking about rationing. Then I thought, "How long would they work our hours for what we are paid?" That waitress got no tip.

There was always something going on in L.A. Edie and I would stay at the Hayward Hotel whenever possible because they were especially good to Service women. They handed out postcards at the desk, with a picture on the front of the Elizabeth Arden Powder Room. On the back it read: "The Elizabeth Arden

Powder Room at the Service Women's Center in the Hayward Hotel, Los Angeles, California, where girls in the service of the United Nations are welcome, one of the several sponsored by the National Fraternity, Kappa Kappa Gamma."

Elizabeth Arden Powder Room

This was a beautiful room. Elizabeth Arden kept it supplied with samples of everything in makeup and perfume that anyone would desire. We could try different makeup, which we did, and go to stores and purchase what we liked. There were lounge chairs where one could relax or read if we chose.

If we had dates, and we did most of the time, we would meet after we had settled into our hotels, go to the USO to check out what was going on in L.A., and get free tickets to shows, if there were any. There were some great stage shows. If we didn't have dates when we arrived, there were a lot of lonely sailors looking for someone to spend time with. This is how we found Clifton's

Cafeteria. A group of us came out of our hotel and were surrounded by a bunch of Corpsmen from Corona.

One of them, whom I knew, came up to me and said, "Have you had lunch? We have found this great restaurant just down the street, called Clifton's Cafeteria. We were going there. How about joining us?"

We all agreed and were delighted that we had. The food was good, but the best part was the music. We walked in and saw a raised stage with a pianist at a grand piano accompanying a soloist who was singing opera. My friend explained that all the waiters and waitresses sang or played an instrument, or both. They were all starving artists hoping to be discovered. All you had to do was request a song. You could choose which waiter or waitress you wanted to hear, or they would choose for you. We heard everything from blues to opera. It was wonderful. We made this our regular stop every time we went to L.A., until the Actors Union made them stop letting the waiters perform. What a shame! They were doing a great job entertaining troops.

After lunch, we headed for the Studio Club Guest House in Hollywood for tickets to stage or radio shows, ending up at the Palladium. We danced to the music of Tommy Dorsey. Big bands always played here, and we went frequently. It was so crowded that you were forced to dance in a circle around the room. The band was so loud that you couldn't carry on a conversation. We danced until we had to leave to catch the last street car back to our hotels.

CHAPTER 9

My Friend Joe

O ne of my patients, a seventeen-year-old Marine, told me he had lied about his age to get into the Service. When this was discovered, he was on his way to Guadalcanal. It was hard to believe he could have fooled them, he was so young looking. In this story I will call him Joe.

Joe was being treated for malaria. He told me how homesick he was and how he just wanted to go home. I listened as he followed me around the ward, helping me in any way he could. He wanted to talk about his experiences in the Service. He had already been through hell and back, yet he was still a child.

When the chow cart came, Joe was always there to help. I had just finished serving the trays when one of my Marine patients had a severe malaria attack. We moved him into a private room at the end of the ward, and I was left to care for him. His chills were so severe, they shook the room.

Joe stayed with me, helping pile blankets on the patient until the chills stopped and the fever started. Then we used ice packs and cold cloths to bring the fever down. He was hallucinating.

While I was bathing the patient's face with a cold cloth, he grabbed both my wrists in an iron grip: he was back on the

Battlefield. Joe, standing beside me, tried to help as he yelled for his friends on the ward. Suddenly the room was filled with Marines. They had to pry his fingers loose from my arms. When the fever broke, the patient had no memory of what had happened, and none of us told him. I don't know what would have happened if Joe had not been there.

One early afternoon, Joe rushed up to me and said "Andy, there is a patient back there, bleeding. He said not to bother you, but I think you should take a look at him."

The nurse had stepped off the ward and the other Corpsmen had gone to lunch. I followed Joe back to the bed where the patient was holding his nose with a blood-soaked handkerchief. I sent Joe to the galley for ice and a pan of water while I gathered up cloths and bandages. When the patient took the handkerchief away, blood gushed out. He was hemorrhaging. I gave him a clean, ice-cold cloth and showed him how to apply pressure to try to stop the bleeding while I rushed to the phone to call the doctor.

The on-call doctor was at lunch. His nurse said they would try to reach him and send him up. I went back to my patient and changed the ice pack. He was still bleeding.

I knew what should be done and how to do it. He needed to have his nose packed but I was only allowed to do this with a nurse or doctor supervising. I felt I had no choice. I had to do something, so I packed his nose with gauze and stopped the bleeding. I cleaned up the blood and changed his bed.

About that time, the doctor arrived. He checked the patient, removed the packing, and repacked the nose. When he finished, he stood up, looked at me, and asked, "Who packed this patient's nose?"

"I did, Sir," I confessed. He could see there was no one else there who could have done it.

The doctor looked at me and said sternly, "You know that is Court-Martial offense, don't you Corpsman?" Without waiting for an answer, his stern look changed into a broad smile. He patted me on my shoulder and said, "But you did a hell of a job, Miss Anderson," and he left. I dropped into the first chair I could find. I was exhausted and relieved that I hadn't lost my first patient or been Court-Martialed.

Corpsmen took turns going to lunch. I was on the ward when the chow cart arrived, so it was my responsibility to put the food out to those who weren't able to go to the mess hall. Joe was always there to help me. One day he said, "Andy, I think I am cracking up."

I said, "Joe you aren't cracking up. What makes you think that you are?"

"Well, I am having headaches and they tell me that is a sign. I have seen a lot of guys crack up and that is the way it starts." I asked if he had talked with the nurse or his doctor about it. He said, "I hate nurses, but I talked to the doctor and he prescribed aspirin, but it hasn't helped.

Later, I spoke to the nurse and she checked his chart. She found that a doctor had put Joe on Atabrine for malaria. It was a drug that you started on a low dose, built up to a maximum dose and then brought it down gradually. Someone had made a mistake. They took him up to the high dose and didn't bring him down until I alerted the nurse that something was wrong. Obviously, no one had checked his chart. She immediately started lowering the dose, but the damage had been done.

The next day, I reported to sickbay. I had a bronchial infection and was admitted to the hospital as a patient. I worried about Joe. I felt he was very fragile and I knew he didn't like nurses for some unknown reason.

I received a message from the ward that Joe was upset that I hadn't come on duty on the ward. The head nurse asked that I be allowed to come to the ward to assure Joe that I was okay. Because of my bronchial infection, the doctor would not allow me to go.

Joe apparently became very angry when a nurse tried to talk with him, and he threw her over a bed. He was placed in a straight-jacket and transported to San Diego to the psychiatric ward.

When I heard this, I cried. Joe was like a little brother. He had seen and done things that would have broken many men and he had survived only to end up in a psychiatric ward, perhaps because of a medical error. I said many prayers for Joe that he would be treated well and would recover. One of the sad things in my work was that, when a patient left the hospital, we had no way of following their lives. Perhaps that was a good thing.

CHAPTER 10

Unit II and Mr. Richardson

When I was released from the hospital October 7, I was assigned to the Postoperative Ward. I had been hoping for this assignment ever since I got to Corona. I had been on the Malaria Ward, the Orthopedic Ward and finally Postop. I hadn't been there a day when orders came from Captain Jenson for me to report to Unit No II, the TB Unit, at 0800 on October 8, 1943.

Unit II was located in the valley one mile below Unit I, the main hospital and my quarters. I didn't mind the walk morning and evening, except when it rained. At least the road was graveled, so I didn't have trouble with mud. The Fire Station was right next to our quarters. I could catch a ride on a fire truck that shook itself down to Unit II every morning. I would walk back in the evening. I only took advantage of the truck in bad weather.

I was a little nervous when I reported to Captain E.G. Brian. He welcomed me to Unit II and told me that I was the first WAVE to be assigned to the TB Unit. "I hope you will be happy here with us," he said as he ushered me across the hall to the Records Office to meet my new Boss, Mr. Richardson.

Mr. Richardson was a Warrant Officer. He looked exactly like Clark Gable, right down to his razor-thin mustache. I learned shortly that he thought he was Clark Gable. He was in charge of the Records Office and he was my boss. He introduced me to the two Corpsmen with whom I would be working, assigned me a desk, and explained what I was to do.

Dr. Miano and Mr. Richardson

All the patients were bed patients and not allowed to leave the ward. Many would never go home.

I loved my job here except for "CLARK GABLE." He would sit with his feet on the desk and stare at me. Then he started dangling a set of keys and saying, "Want my key?" I politely told him I had no use for his key, nor did I want it. This didn't stop him.

One day I told him I thought officers were supposed to be gentlemen. His response was, "I am a gentleman. I am an officer and a gentleman by Act of Congress."

My co-workers thought this harassment was funny, but they let me know I had gained their respect. I was now one of them.

Mr. Richardson kept a bottle of C.P. (chemically pure) alcohol in his desk drawer and frequently sipped from it. The Corpsmen working with me had nicknamed him C.P.

We ate our lunches in the Unit-II Mess Hall, but I would go topside for dinner, especially for Thanksgiving and Christmas, when we were served gourmet dinners.

My hours were better there. I worked 8 hours a day, but when I left the office in the evening on my duty day, I was on call at any time I was needed. I could be called to special a patient for four hours on and four hours off. We could also be called to admit new patients. There wasn't a time limit on that. You worked until all patients were assigned to wards, regardless of the time it took.

I was called for Special Duty only once. They assigned me to special a Marine that had been severely burned. His plane had crashed and burst into flames. He was the sole survivor. People nearby tried to help him, but the flames drove them back. He walked out of the plane on fire and collapsed. They were able to put out the flames by the time the ambulance arrived. He was then transported to the Corona Naval Hospital Intensive Care Unit. He had third-degree burns over much of his body.

As I approached his room, I was almost overcome by the odor. I had never before smelled burned, festering, human flesh. The odor was so overwhelming, I could taste it. To this day, when I think about this patient, I remember that stench. It is an odor I have never been able to forget.

I was not prepared for what hit me when I entered the patient's room. His face was unrecognizable. His ears and nose were gone. The patient had a broken back and was in a full-body cast. There were holes cut in the cast so I could apply medication to the burned area.

The part of his body not in a cast was covered in bandages which were to be kept moist with the medication. The patient was in an induced coma. IVs had been set up by the nurse who, before leaving, gave me instructions on how and when to apply the medications. I carefully followed instructions and watched for any change in his condition as I prayed for his recovery.

When I was relieved, four hours later, I rushed back to my room and into the shower, trying to get rid of that horrible odor that still lingered in my hair, my nostrils and clothing.

The next morning I was back at my job in the Records Office, but I followed the progress of this patient, visiting him frequently. He was very fortunate. We had a group of doctors from the Mayo Clinic, who worked as a unit. There were specialists in all fields and they accepted a salary of only $1.00 a year.

One of the specialists was a plastic surgeon. By performing multiple skin grafts over many months, this doctor was able to rebuild the patient's face by using an old snapshot provided by the patient's girlfriend.

One of my jobs in the Records Office was to enter information into the patients' files. We could not help becoming interested in them. I discovered that many of the patients here had been assigned to the same ship. The personnel on that ship had all been tested for TB before boarding ship, but they had not yet received the results when the ship was deployed. When it was discovered a sailor assigned to the galley had active TB, it was too late to alert the Captain because of radio communication blackouts. By the time the ship returned to Port, many of the crew had become infected.

We who worked in Unit II had to be checked every three months for TB and were told we should be checked every six months for two years after leaving the Unit.

My brother Wayne and I had kept in touch. I wrote him several times a week and he would respond. Postage was free for Service personnel. Wayne was stationed at Camp McCall in North Carolina. He wrote, telling me he was being sent to Camp Polk, Louisiana, for swamp maneuvers. This was bad news. It meant he was going to be sent to the Pacific Theater. Anyone, if given a choice, would choose the Atlantic Theater.

I had been working in Unit II for six months when I received a telegram from my mother, telling me that Wayne was being given a leave before shipping out. She asked if I could get a leave at the same time.

I went to the Personnel Office and got the request for leave forms and filled them out. I knew it was a long shot because I wasn't eligible for leave for two months. I filled out the form and took it to my boss. I explained that my brother was in the Glider

Infantry and was getting his last leave before shipping out to the Pacific.

He smiled and dangled his keys. "Take my key and I will give you leave."

The look on his face made me sick to my stomach. I turned and sat down at my desk, thinking he would relent, but instead he left the office with a satisfied look on his face.

I kept a jar of candy on my desk and shared it with the office. The Captain was a nice guy. His office was just across the hall and he came into our office every day. He would hold up his hand and say, "At ease, you don't need to stand, go on with your work." He would sit on the corner of my desk, help himself to my candy, and chat with us.

I still had my leave request on my desk, and he saw it. "Do you want a leave, Miss Anderson?" he asked.

I explained about my brother. The Captain picked up my pen, signed the request, said have a good time with your family, and walked out.

When Mr. Richardson returned, he saw the signed leave request on my desk. He was furious. He accused me of going over his head. He didn't listen when I tried to explain, but went storming out.

In less than an hour, a runner from the Personnel Office came in and handed me orders to report to the Fire Department. I was to replace a WAVE who had been given leave because of a death in the family. This cancelled my leave. I knew C.P. had gone to his buddy in the Personnel Office and arranged this. I wired my mother and told her I had been denied leave.

I reported for duty at the Fire Station the next morning and tried to concentrate on the new job. I was the secretary at the Fire Department. I AM NO SECRETARY! The Fire Chief was a friend of Mr. Richardson, both old-time Regular Navy men. They had been promoted in rank when the war broke out.

I had been in my new job two days and hadn't even become familiar with the office routine when someone from the Personnel Office delivered a telegram to me. When I opened it, I found it was from the Red Cross, stating that I had been granted a thirty-day emergency leave, beginning immediately. My mother had appealed to the Red Cross for help. I was amazed that she would know how to work the system and appeal to the Red Cross. I didn't even know how to do that.

I rushed to the barracks, packed, and left that afternoon on the Santa Fe Railroad out of San Bernardino, for Chicago. I would be traveling four nights and four days in coach to Chicago where I could transfer to the Monon Train to Monticello and home.

CHAPTER 11

Train Trip Home On Leave

S ometime between three and four in the afternoon, I boarded the train. I chose a seat on the right side of the train, hoping to see the sunset in the desert.

Fortunately, the train out of San Bernardino was not crowded, allowing me to find a double seat where I would be able to stretch out. The anticipation of visiting my family, for the first time in uniform, outweighed the inconvenience of traveling coach. Pullman was too expensive and I am not sure there were any Pullman cars on the train.

There were several Service men on board, but I was the only Service woman that I saw. There were three Marines who obviously had been drinking heavily and were getting loud and obnoxious. The drunkest got up and started down the aisle. When he spotted me, he called out to his friends. "Hey guys!" he shouted. "A WAVE. 'Join The Navy and ride the WAVES.' We should have joined the Navy, guys." By this time he was standing over me, laughing. I wanted to slap his face, but I turned my face to the window, trying to ignore him and concentrate on the scenery as we wound up through the San Gorgonio Pass. His friends pulled him away and they went on to the next car.

One of the Marines returned about an hour later and sat in the seat across from me. "I want to apologize for my friend," he said. "He is drunk. I know that is no excuse, but he is just back from combat and he is celebrating. He is on medication, and the doctors told him if he drank, it could kill him. We have been trying to keep him from drinking. I threw his bottle out the window, and when he couldn't find it, he went looking for the Club Car. That's when he saw you. I hope you won't judge all Marines by his rudeness."

I looked at him and replied, "You know, I have cared for many sailors and Marines. They had all just come out of combat. I was never insulted by any of them. I am sorry, but I find it difficult to excuse him or his inexcusable behavior."

"I don't blame you. I just want you to know that I respect you and your uniform. I am very sorry this happened. Marines would fight to the death for our Corpsmen. I hope you won't judge all Marines by him."

As I looked at him, sitting there trying to apologize for his friend, I felt sorry for him and said, "I appreciate you apologizing for your friend. I hope he appreciates your friendship. I won't judge all Marines by him. I do thank you for coming back to talk to me."

He smiled and offered his hand. I took it and forced a smile in return, but I still felt angry and humiliated. I turned to the window and tried to forget the whole incident as I enjoyed the scenery. There is nothing like a desert sunset.

Around ten, they dimmed the lights and I curled up, using my purse as a pillow and my Regulation raincoat/overcoat as a cover, and slept.

In the middle of the night, I was startled by someone touching my shoulder. When I opened my eyes, there were two Military Policemen standing over me. I assumed they wanted to see my traveling orders, but before I could produce them, one of the men spoke, "Are you a Corpsman?"

"Yes, I am. What is the problem?"

"We need your help. We have a very sick Serviceman back in the next car. Please follow us."

I picked up my purse and followed them. I was praying, "Dear Lord, please don't let it be that horrible drunk Marine."

We went through the next car and through the rear door to the small platform outside the car. It was he, curled up in a fetal position next to the guard rails that surrounded the platform. His friends were there, keeping him from falling off. I am sure they had told the MPs where to find me.

They were looking at me, expecting me to fix him. My Corps School didn't include treating drunks. I was trying to think of what to do when I remembered one of my Corpsman friends telling me how he had forced a drunk Marine to drink warm salt water until he vomited.

I looked at the drunk Marine and back at the MPs, and said, "I don't know if I can help him. His friends told me earlier that he was mixing alcohol with his medications. He is in bad shape."

One of the MPs spoke up, "You tell us what to do and we will see that it is done."

"You have to get him to empty his stomach. Go to the Club Car and get a lot of warm salt water and make him drink it until he vomits. If that doesn't work, you had better get him off the train at the next stop and get him to a doctor."

One of the Marines thanked me and took off for the Club Car for the salt water.

"Please let me know if I can be of further help," I said as I turned to leave.

The MPs thanked me and one of them insisted on seeing me back to my seat.

I settled in, but I couldn't sleep. What if my advice didn't work? As obnoxious as he had been to me, I wanted him to live and I knew he might not. I prayed for him until sleep took over.

The next day, after breakfast, I was in my seat reading a book when someone sat down in the seat across from me. I looked up and there he was. He looked pale, but he was stone sober.

"I don't know where to start," he said. "I want to thank you for helping me last night. I wouldn't have blamed you if you hadn't. My friends told me how I talked to you. All I can say is I am sorry. Being drunk was no excuse. I hope you will accept my apology."

I looked at him and said, "I took care of you because it was my duty as a Corpsman. I honor your uniform."

He replied, "No one will ever say anything against a WAVE to me after last night. I want you to know that I honor your uniform. Please accept my apology. I believe you saved my life. I haven't seen my family for over a year. I can't thank you enough for making that possible."

"I am not sure that it was my treatment that saved your life, but I accept your apology. I must admit, however, I did get a lot of satisfaction out of thinking of you drinking that warm salt water and heaving up your insides." We both laughed.

"The train is pulling into the station. This is where I get off," he said. He stood, snapped to attention, and saluted me smartly.

"God bless the WAVES," he said, loud enough for the other passengers to hear, as he turned and left the train.

The rest of the trip was uneventful. I changed trains in Chicago, taking the Monon train to Monticello, Indiana. Everyone was at the station to meet me. My mother stood smiling as she watched me step out of the door. It was great to see my family again.

CHAPTER 12

Visiting Heroes

My little sisters, Josephine 8, Lois 10, and brother Bob 12, stood close to their big brother. They were beaming with pride. Wayne and I might not be heroes to anyone else, but that day we were heroes to our siblings.

Wayne looked sharp in his army uniform with the Glider insignia on his cap. He rushed to help me off the train with my luggage and gave me a big hug. He had grown two inches since he went into the Service. My little brother was now taller than me.

My little brother, Wayne

Wayne had been stationed at Camp Polk, Louisiana, and had just completed Swamp Maneuvers. His face was as red as his hair and covered with blisters that had scabbed over. He reminded me of the soldiers I had seen from the Troop Train in the California desert.

As we walked the two blocks home from the station, Wayne told me the Kiwanis club had invited us to speak at their luncheon meeting.

Bob excitedly told me his teacher, Mrs. Huston, had asked us to visit and speak to her sixth grade class. His teacher had taught all nine of his older siblings, but at that time she was Miss Young. During the Depression, in Indiana and many other states, women teachers were not hired if they were married. If they were hired and decided to get married, they were let go. Teaching jobs were reserved for men or single women. This restriction was lifted during the war because the men teachers left for wartime jobs or joined the Service. Miss Young had been secretly married for some time. Now she could go by her married name without fear of losing her job.

Mom put the girls to work setting the table while Bob did his chores and she got dinner ready. This gave Wayne and me a chance to catch up on each other's experiences. He told about spending days tramping through swamps. As he was talking, he fell asleep in the middle of a word. He was completely exhausted and sleep deprived.

When he awakened, we laughed about it. He said, "While in the swamp we got very little sleep; some days, we got none. There was no dry place to lie down. One day, I was so sleepy that when I saw a half-submerged log, I stretched out on it and fell sound asleep. At that point, I was so tired I didn't care what was slithering through the water. That was where I got sunburned."

Mom had fixed her famous fried chicken, mashed potatoes, gravy and vegetables. She had saved her sugar rations to make us an apple pie.

While we ate, no one talked about the war. Mom showed none of the anxiety we knew she felt. Every meal was special while we were home.

Mom told us all the news about the family. She had made plans for us to go visit her Uncle Chester Wickersham and his daughter Ruth, for whom I was named. "I know you will want to visit and decorate Papa's grave," she said, "and on the way, we can stop at Aunt Mae's and visit for awhile." We went everyplace Mom wanted to go and treasured every minute we spent together.

Monday morning, we went to school with Bob. Mrs. Huston greeted us warmly and said, "Class, I am going to let Bob Anderson introduce our guest speakers this morning."

Bob stepped up, proudly introduced us to his class, and then took a seat near the back of the room.

Ruth and Wayne

Wayne spoke first, telling about his basic training, what it was like flying in Gliders. They were fascinated about his stories of the swamp maneuvers he had just completed. Wide-eyed students peppered him with questions.

When I spoke, I told them stories about some of my patients and how we treated their wounds, leaving out the gory details. The girls wanted to know what it was like being in the WAVES. It was fun watching their faces as we spoke, but even more fun watching my little brother's proud smile.

We were treated as visiting heroes in Monticello, our small home town of 3500 people, where we knew most everyone. Everywhere we went, Wayne and I shook hands or were embraced by old friends and well-wishers. We learned about our many friends and classmates who were serving, missing in action, or had been killed in combat. All through the town, we saw Blue or Gold Star Flags hanging in windows. The local newspaper had already printed an article about our homecoming, and everyone was happy to see us and ask questions.

Wayne took me to the Kiwanis luncheon. They all knew Wayne and his sense of humor. They expected a good laugh and weren't disappointed. He could have been a stand-up comedian. Wayne spoke in more detail about his training and added funny things that happened in camp and on maneuvers, leaving everyone laughing. He should have followed me because my talk wasn't funny. He hadn't yet seen the results of war.

I gave them a brief rundown on my training in classes and on the job, but they had more interest in the patients and their treatment. They wanted to hear details about Jungle Rot and treatment our boys got on the field and after they reached our hospital.

I expected to speak for a very short time, but they asked dozens of questions. They were hungry for first-hand news about the war. I tried to answer their questions, avoiding negative things. I knew most of them had boys in the Service and I didn't want to add to their worries. I am sure they were all late getting back to work.

On the way home, Wayne asked more questions. I stressed how important it was for him to keep his feet dry to avoid Jungle Rot. (He told me later that he kept a dry pair of socks tied to his uniform all the time he was on the Islands.) I told him some of the Marines had gone swimming in the ocean and cut their feet on coral. They thought that also caused their foot problems.

We stopped at the drugstore where I used to work and had a soda. As we started to leave, I picked up a packet of stationery. It was a pack with three different colors of paper. I bought it, paid for our drinks, and we headed home.

I handed Wayne the stationary and said, "When you write me, write on the white paper. If you go into combat, write me on the pink paper. When you get out of combat, write on the green paper. That way I will know where you are without endangering anyone."

Wayne laughed and promised he would keep our code a secret.

Our 30-day leave passed too quickly. We never had a chance to say all the things we wanted to say. When Wayne put me on the train, we hugged and I whispered, "Keep your head down, Little Brother. Don't try to be a hero."

He laughed that musical laugh of his and said, "Don't worry. I am the best shot in my Company."

I took a seat by the window and watched him standing by our mother until they were out of view. They couldn't see the tears in my eyes as the train pulled out. I knew what he would be facing and I prayed for God to protect my little brother.

CHAPTER 13

Property and Accounting

U pon arriving back at the hospital after my leave, I reported to the Personnel Office for my new Duty Assignment. I looked at the assignment and was terrified. I was to report to the Orthopedic Department to act as secretary to an Orthopedic Surgeon. I AM NOT A SECRETARY!

I reported as ordered. The surgeon to whom I was assigned was from the Mayo Clinic. His short body was all legs. My job was to follow him through the wards, take notes on each patient, and transfer those notes to permanent records. I have a long stride, but to keep up with him I almost had to run. Not only did he walk fast, but he spoke as fast as he walked and I didn't know shorthand.

When a Marine or sailor had an arm or leg fracture on the battlefield, Corpsmen would fill the wound with sulfa powder to prevent infection, put a cast on it, and go to the next patient. There wasn't time to clean the wound first. The patient was then moved to a hospital ship and sent back to the states as soon as possible. When they reached our hospital, we removed the casts to clean the wounds of leaves and other debris that had been left there. Thank God for sulfa powder.

I stood with the doctor and watched this procedure. I would have loved working with this doctor as a Corpsman, but not as a secretary. We went from bed to bed, checking on patients' progress, charting those who needed surgery, removing casts or replacing casts, and ordering treatment for them. I think we hit every orthopedic ward in that huge hospital. When we finished, he headed to surgery, leaving me to decipher my notes and record them. After three days of this, I knew I had to do something.

One of my friends, Rita Kizis, worked in the Property and Accounting Department. On the way home, I stopped by her room and told her my problem. She said a Corpsman in the Equipment Office had just received orders to ship out; they would need someone to replace him. Her roommate Alice, who worked in the Personnel Office suggested, "Andy, go to the Personnel Office and explain the situation to the officer in charge. Tell them you had heard there was an opening in Property and Management and request that you be considered for that position. After you leave, I will tell them I know you and feel you would be great in that job."

"Oh, thank you, Alice. I will go there first thing in the morning. You will know before I do whether I get the assignment or not."

I got up early the next morning. Hurrying through breakfast, I rushed down to the Personnel Office and asked to speak to the head of Personnel. I was sitting there waiting when Alice came in. She spoke to her boss and then motioned me over and introduced me.

"Alice tells me you would like to be reassigned. What is your problem with your present assignment?" he asked.

"Well Sir, to begin with, I am not a secretary. I don't take short-hand and have had no secretarial experience. I am afraid I will make a mistake in charting that might endanger one of the patients. I have been told there is an opening in Property and Accounting and I feel I could do a good job there, Sir." It worked. They reassigned me. God had to be looking after me and my patients.

I took my orders and reported to my new assignment. This was the best job I had in the Navy. It was a large department on two floors. Navy and Civilian personnel worked together. The Supply Department was on the ground floor and Equipment Department, just above it, on the second floor. This was where I reported to work. There was a Lieutenant, whom we seldom saw, in charge of both departments. My immediate boss was a Warrant Officer, Mr. Anderson, whom everyone called Andy (two Andy's in the same office?). He was a Reserve Officer and a great boss.

Part of the gang at Property & Accounting

Most of the Corpsmen working in Equipment were in their late thirties. The Draft Boards were running out of young men. Austin Horn, married with two children, owned a dry-cleaning company in Sulphur, Oklahoma. Floyd Hinman, from Vermont, brought his wife Peg and Daughter Virginia to live near the base. Gus Mueller was from New York (his family owned the Mueller Instrument factory). C.L. Cairns was from Mansfield, Ohio. Tony Giacobbi was from the East Coast (his father owned a fruit and vegetable market). Rita Kizis and I were the only WAVES in the office. This was a great crew. They treated me like a younger sister. Roy Nilmeier, Postmaster from Fresno, California, was one of our gang. He ran the Hospital Post Office.

Then there was Vern West. He was thirty-eight and had a home in L.A. His wife, Rose, worked in a defense plant. They had no children and sort of adopted me. Rose would ask Vern to bring any of us home with him when we had weekend passes. Frequently, if I had nothing planned, I would go with him. Rose would not be home when we arrived, so Vern would take us to their favorite neighborhood spots and introduce us to all their friends. By the time we got back to his house, Rose would have dinner on the table.

Rose and Vern West

After a couple of visits to their home, while helping clean up after dinner, I said, "Rose, when I visit you, I feel guilty. You come home after working all day, and fix dinner for all of us. We get here early and I would love to fix dinner for you. I will call you when we get here and you can tell me what you have planned; or just leave me a note and I will check in the refrigerator and have dinner ready when you got home."

Rose gave me a hug and said, "I would love that, thank you so much. It will give us more time to visit or go out together. I can't remember when someone cooked for me. What a treat that will be." I dearly loved this couple.

The wives of our shipmates and the ladies who worked in our offices were about the only civilians with whom we had any contact. There were two lady civilian workers in the Equipment

Office and several in the Supply Office. They mothered us all. They all had cars and were generous about giving us rides.

Our job was to keep track of all the equipment on the base. One morning I had a call from Intensive Care, asking for an electric fan for a critically ill patient. I checked and found there were only five fans in the whole hospital. I traced down their locations and found two were in use in Critical Care and the rest were in Captain Jensen's quarters. All factories had been converted to manufacturing war equipment, so there were no fans to be purchased.

I asked Mr. Anderson, "Should I call Mrs. Jenson and explain the need for a fan and see if she will give us one?"

He laughed and said, "Go ahead, but I can tell you, you won't get one". Everyone in the office listened as I made the call. I explained the situation and told her there were only five fans in the hospital and perhaps she would let us have one of the three she had, for a short time. It was needed for a critically ill patient.

She was furious, "How dare you call me and ask for one of 'my fans'?" She slammed the phone down. I was glad I hadn't given her my name. The poor patient never got his fan, but I had tried.

The Lieutenant in charge of Property and Accounting received an Order from the 11Th Naval District Headquarters in San Diego. We were to locate all motorized equipment assigned to the base and provide this information to Headquarters.

The Lieutenant assigned this job to me. I felt like a private eye. Going through our records, I followed each piece of equipment by its assigned number and recorded location. I called the departments to which they had been assigned. In most cases I would find it had been reassigned to another department without going through our office. I found a truck and a large piece of earthmoving equipment on a ranch belonging to one of the officers. He had borrowed this equipment some time back and apparently everyone was afraid to request its return.

I asked the Lieutenant what I should do. He said, "Well, we know where it is." I took this to mean report it as being located on the base. This bothered me. The following day he came to me and asked, "Miss Anderson, do you have your inventory completed?"

"Yes Sir".

"Good, I want you to accompany me to the 11ᵗʰ Naval District Headquarters to make your report. I will pick you up here tomorrow morning at 0700."

After breakfast the next morning, I went to the office where I found another Corpsman waiting. He had a report to deliver from the Supply Office.

The Lieutenant picked us up and we traveled south for two or three hours through orange groves, dairy farms and small towns. When we got into San Diego, I recognized Balboa Park and the San Diego Naval Hospital as we passed. The 11ᵗʰ Naval District Headquarters was located in a large building on the edge of the harbor. The Lieutenant ushered us into an office and introduced us to the Warrant Officer who was to take our reports. He said, "I will pick you up after lunch when you have finished your reporting," and he left.

The Corpsman from Supply gave his inventory report first. When it was my turn, I gave a complete report, including the location of the missing equipment. I wondered if anything would be done about it or if I would be in trouble. When we finished, we had lunch with the enlisted personnel and waited for our boss to return to pick us up.

We got back to the base around 5:00 p.m. (1700 Navy time). I was greeted by a bunch of smiling Corpsmen and Mr. Anderson. The missing equipment had been delivered back onto the base and its locations had been logged in.

Several weeks later, Gus came to me and said he and I had been chosen to take an inventory of the contents in a huge walk-in vault. This vault contained everything of value left from the Norconian Country Club. He had been told there was a lot of silverware along with table linens and expensive glassware and serving dishes. This inventory should have been done before the government took over, but getting the hospital up and running had taken priority.

We knew much of what had been there had walked, and Gus was concerned that they were looking for someone to blame when our inventory was matched to that of the former owners. He said, "I am going to tell them we will be glad to do the job, but we want to be searched each time we enter the vault and when we leave." I would never have given this a thought and appreciated Gus taking care of me. After he made his request, we never heard anything more about an inventory of the vault.

CHAPTER 14

Letters from Wayne

I wrote Wayne several times a week and he would write back funny, upbeat letters. Each time I wrote, I would end the letter with, "Keep your head down and your feet dry, little brother."

When he shipped out, we got no letters until he arrived in New Guinea, where he was training in gliders. He wrote, "I have just found out that Paratroopers get flight pay. I am trying to decide whether to transfer to the Paratroopers. Gliders are sitting ducks in the air once they are released from the plane. Paratroopers are targets as they float down to earth. They both end up behind enemy lines. What a choice!"

Wayne had made his decision. He wrote, "I have decided to go for the money. If I am a target anyway, I might as well get paid for it. I have to make three jumps to qualify. If I fail to jump the third jump, I will be back in the Gliders. If I make the third jump, there is no turning back."

In his next letter he said, "Well Ruth, I managed to make the first two jumps. I was a little worried when I went up for the third, but that was the easiest of all. When it came time to jump, I was so airsick I didn't care if it killed me. I wanted out of that plane and on solid ground. Your little brother has qualified and is now a Paratrooper and $50 richer each month."

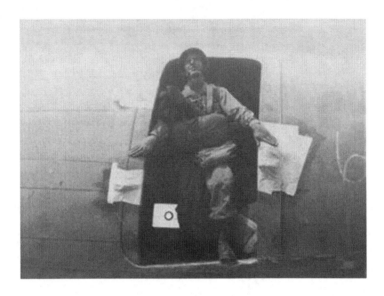

Paratrooper Wayne Anderson

Changing from Gliders to the Paratroopers no doubt extended his training time. He sent pictures of himself, always with that mischievous boyish smile. In one picture he was standing in the door of a plane, ready to jump, and in another with three of his friends, standing in a swamp after a jump. He wrote on the back of this picture: "Taken after my last jump in New Guinea. They took me for a ride five times in a plane and I had to walk home each time. I wonder how it feels to land in a plane. Incidentally, that is me on the right of the four."

Wayne's last jump in New Guinea

MEET IN NEW GUINEA

Four local youths recently enjoyed a reunion together in New Guinea. Cpl. Leland Foreman and Pfc. Wayne Anderson, who are stationed in New Guinea, hearing there were two Monticello boys in a camp a short distance away, had a pleasant surprise at seeing Jack Curbox and Sgt. Truman Randall. They had dinner together and spent the afternoon together talking over old times and the old home town.

Monticello Herald Journal

Would Like Some Chickens From Home

Mrs. Geo. Mecum, R. 4, Monticello, has received from Pfc. Wayne (Red) Anderson, the following reply to an ad which she had placed in the Herald-Journal in reference to some fries which she had to sell:

Dear Mrs. Mecum:

I just ran across your ad in the paper that you have fries for sale. I'll take two, around four pounds if possible and due to the present conditions, I won't be able to come after them. I'd prefer them to be deliverd. Just have George drop them off at my back door and while you are at it, you might as well bring a few more. I'm sure my neighbors will patronize you also. Leave them at the sixth tent on the right, New Guinea.

"Red."

Monticello Herald Journal

Then the dreaded letter came, written on pink paper. I was able to read some of it, but it looked like a lace doily where words had been cut out by the Censors. I knew he was going into combat because he wrote it on pink paper and I knew he would be in the jungle because his last sentence was, "Don't worry. I am keeping my feet dry." I learned later that he had been in combat on the Island of Leyte.

I waited for weeks for his next letter. When it came, it was written on a piece of brown paper bag. I learned many months later that he had picked it up on the battlefield. He said, "I am out of the green paper you gave me and this is the only thing I could find." I thanked God my little brother was out of combat.

Our letters continued back and forth and my life continued as usual. I enrolled in classes again for a step-up in rate to first class. I studied hard, passed the test, and was surprised when they told me that, although I received one of the highest grades, I would have to wait for my stripes. There were only so many openings for PHM1/c, and those slots would be given to the male Corpsmen who had passed the test, regardless of how well they had scored. When the last man got his rate, the WAVES who had passed the test would get their stripes, based on grades. I was disappointed that gender took precedence over grades, but I accepted the decision as fair. After all, the men were the ones who went through hell if and when they were shipped out.

I received another letter from Wayne, telling me he was out of pink paper. He said, "It wasn't my head that got it that second day on _____." I had to wait for the war to end with Japan to get the cutouts filled in.

CHAPTER 15

The War Was Intensifying

*I*n late August, we received a shipment of patients from Saipan. I had already worked 8 hours in my office and was in the Chow Hall when the order came over the loudspeakers, "All available Corpsmen report topside to admit patients." I rushed through dinner and reported as ordered.

It seemed each group that came in was in worse shape than the last. The patients were assigned to certain wards according to their particular injuries. We took them to their assigned ward and saw that they were registered in before returning for the next patient. It was after 0200 before I got to my room, showered, and slipped into bed. Sleep usually came quickly from sheer exhaustion, but many times it was a restless sleep with dreams of broken bodies and caring for the wounded.

This would be repeated more frequently as the war intensified. We were receiving new patients every day, and more and more Corpsmen were getting orders to ship out.

In early November, Walter Hendricks, the Corpsman whom I had been dating for several weeks, received his orders. Before he was to ship out, he asked me to marry him. I loved him, but it was the love of a dear friend, not the love he felt for me. I told him,

"Walter, you know I really care for you, but I promised myself I would wait until the end of the war to make such an important decision. When you get back, we will see if we have the same feeling for each other as we do now. Ask me then." It was a very sad goodbye, but he accepted my decision: not as a "No," but as a "Wait-and-see."

Monday morning, I reported to my office with a heavy heart. Sending a dear friend off to battle was different in the Service than in civilian life: we saw the horrors of war daily. There was no standing by a train and waving goodbye. For security reasons, those shipping out weren't told exactly when they would be leaving the base or where they were being sent. I didn't know when Walter left the base.

The next weekend, Edie and I went to L.A. We got tickets from the USO to see the opera, "Porgy and Bess." It was wonderful. Saturday night, we had tickets for the Ice Follies. The skating was unbelievable and the costumes were magnificent. We got in very late, and Edie had to be on the wards early the next morning.

When I returned to my room that evening, I found Edie stretched out on her bed, sobbing uncontrollably. She had received a Dear Jane letter from the man she had been engaged to since 1941, before the war began. He was in the Army and had been in combat in the European Theater. He was the reason she had joined the Service. The letter had come from a base hospital. Picking it up, while trying to control her voice, Edie read a paragraph, "I am no longer the person you knew. I have been so badly injured, I will never marry anyone. Please forget me, find someone who can give you a life. Don't try to see me or contact me. It is best for both of us." I was holding her and crying with her. After that, Edie changed. She was never the same. It was sad to watch.

Walter and I exchanged letters for a few weeks. His last letter said, "I don't know when I will be able to write again, but pray for me. I will write when I can." I anxiously checked the mail every day, but I never heard from him after that. I didn't know if his ship had been sunk or if he had been lost in combat. It was like losing a brother. This was the second time this had happened to me, but I knew my decision had been right.

Work went on as usual. Everyone was trying to cheer me up. Some of the guys from the office had discovered an old dude ranch near Norco. It was called Fuller's Ranch and apparently was popular with Service people. Austin Horn suggested we all go there on our next liberty night and check it out.

Roy took Kenny, Vi, Austin, and me in his car. Gus and a friend of his, George Davies, went with Rita, Alice and her Marine friend in his car. We drove out into the country and finally onto the grounds of the Ranch. I had no idea where we were. We approached a beautiful Spanish-style building on a small lake (in Indiana, we would have called it a pond). Entering through an archway in the vine-covered walls, we found ourselves in a large courtyard with a huge Spanish wishing well in the center.

Before we reached the entry to the building, we could hear laughter and music coming from inside. Just inside the huge door to our right was a long bar crowded with Service people, mostly from the hospital, laughing and enjoying themselves. Beyond the bar was a room filled with slot machines that were working overtime, but I didn't see anyone winning. I wondered, "Is gambling legal in California?"

Rita and Alice, with the rest of our gang, caught up with us. As we joined the crowd at the bar, Gus introduced everyone to his friend, George Davies. George was a lot of fun and fit right in. He immediately became one of our gang, and after a while, he and I started dating.

George was from Indiana, a handsome, Scotsman with a ready smile and curly auburn hair. He was a Republican and a Presbyterian. Mom would have approved. We had just started dating when he received his orders. I was beginning to feel like a jinx.

George was sent to San Francisco in preparation for shipping out. He wrote that he was to get one weekend of liberty and asked if I could come meet him. Gus and Rita suggested that we ask Alice and her Marine boyfriend, who just happened to have a car, if they would take us.

We, who didn't smoke, had been saving our rations of free cigarettes for just such an occasion. We had no gas ration stamps, but gas station owners were more than willing to exchange gas for cigarettes which they could sell. Was this Black Market?

We left as soon as we got off on Friday, around 1700. Cigarettes paid for our gas, both ways. It was a long trip up through Los Angeles, through the foothills of the mountains and winding along California's beautiful coastline. It must have been after midnight when we got to San Francisco.

After checking into the Mark Hopkins Hotel, we asked at the desk for messages. There was no message from George. We knew, if he were able, he would have called the hotel. Everyone was disappointed, but decided, since we were in San Francisco, we would make the most of it.

The next morning, we met the guys in the lobby and took the elevator to the Top of the Mark. What a view. We could see all of San Francisco.

We rode the crowded cable car, hanging on for dear life as we careened down steep twisting streets to Fisherman's Wharf. It was quite a thrill. When we got to the Wharf, I was fascinated by the huge steaming crab pots that were amassed along the board-walk in front of restaurants.

Fisherman's Wharf, San Francisco

I watched as they dipped those ugly creatures out of the pots and served them to those brave souls lining the Wharf. I had never seen or eaten crab. They looked too much like giant red spiders to me and I found the smell overwhelming. Instead, we chose to go inside one of the many restaurants, where we had a delicious seafood lunch, after which we took the cable cars all over San Francisco and ended up in Chinatown for a wonderful dinner.

After dinner, Rita asked, "Andy, have you ever heard of Finocchio's? It is a great place to hear good music."

"No, I have never heard of it, but I love good music. Let's go." When we walked in and sat down, the stage was full of beautiful women. I was enjoying listening to an unbelievable soprano solo-ist. Suddenly the voice was a bass. I looked over at my friends to see their reaction, and knew I had been set up.

They were all watching me and laughing at this naive, small-town girl from Indiana. I laughed with them, but thought to my-self, "This wouldn't exist in Indiana."

After the show, we headed back to the hotel. The guys' room was on a different floor from ours. We agreed to meet in the lob-by early the next morning for breakfast, and head home.

In the morning, we entered the elevator. It was packed. When we got off in the lobby, the guys were waiting for us.

Our driver said, "If we drive awhile, we can get ahead of the traffic and it will break up our trip a little." We all agreed to find some place down the coast to eat breakfast.

After driving for a couple hours, we spotted what looked like a nice restaurant and stopped. When I went to pay for my break-fast, I discovered there were no bills in my wallet. There were a couple dollars in change in the coin purse and everything else was there, but no folding money. Someone in that crowded elevator must have slipped my wallet out of my cross-body bag without my even noticing. How they could take the wallet, remove the money and return the wallet without my noticing I will never know. Fortunately, they at least returned the wallet with my I.D. Since I always kept some money in my inside jacket pocket, I was able to pay for my breakfast. I had never been robbed before, and it made me angry. I couldn't believe anyone would rob a Service man or woman.

It was late and we were exhausted when we reached the base. In spite of being robbed and George not showing up, it had been a great liberty weekend. We had missed the Christmas Dance but since Christmas Day fell on a Tuesday, we didn't miss the gift exchanges in our office or the Christmas dinner.

U.S. NAVAL HOSPITAL, CORONA, CALIFORNIA

Christmas Dinner

Crab meat cocktail
Celery hearts   Spiced peaches   Assorted olives
Hard candies   Mixed nuts

Consomme a la Macedoine
Fairy toast   crackers

Roast Young Tom Utah Turkey, dressing, Cranberry Jelley
Baked Sugar Cured Virginia Ham, Pineapple Sauce

Candied Yams   Cream whipped potatoes
Creamed green peas   Buttered carrots

Parker house rolls   Combination salad
Ice cream   Fruit cake   French apple pie
                 cigarettes
      coffee   tea   milk

H.L. JENSEN   J.D. JEWELL
Captain (MC) U.S.Navy   Capt. (MC) U.S.N.
Commanding.   Executive Officer

VIRGIL H. STAMBAUGH
Pharm. (Ret) U.S.N.
Commissary Officer.

Christmas dinner menu

CHAPTER 16

New Year's Eve Dance

*I*t was Saturday, December 30, 1944. The hospital and our quarters were still decorated for Christmas. Sprigs of desert holly and desert mistletoe hung in doorways. A huge, beautifully decorated Christmas tree stood in the lobby of our quarters and another in the lobby of the hospital. The hospital was decorated throughout. It was my Duty weekend, but I didn't mind. Holidays off base were lonelier than on the base with my Navy family, and our Navy cooks were the best.

We looked forward to the Ship's Dance. This would be our New Year's Eve party, although a day early. We knew they would have a great band and our friend, Joe Puccio, would be singing with them.

My roommate Vi with her date, Kenny, and I decided to stop in Ship's Service for a coke before going down to the Ballroom. When we walked in, we saw Rita and Alice with a group of our friends. We were all talking and laughing and I didn't notice the handsome sailor watching me from the other side of the U-shaped counter.

When we had finished our drinks, we all walked out together and down the grand stairway to the Ballroom. My friends went in, but I stopped off at the ladies' room. When I came out into the brightly lit hall and entered the dimly lit Ballroom, I stopped just inside the door to allow my eyes to adjust to the change in lighting. Before I could see, I heard someone say, "May I have this dance?" I turned toward the voice and accepted. I didn't know what he looked like, but he had a nice voice and he wasn't in a cast. When we got out onto the floor where there was more light, I looked up into deep blue, smiling eyes. He was ruggedly handsome with a square jaw and a slightly crooked nose. He was not anyone I had seen before.

"I am Herb Gunther. What is your name?" he asked, smiling down at me.

"Officially, I am Winona Ruth Anderson. The Navy calls me Winona, my Mother calls me Ruth and everyone else calls me Andy. Take your pick."

Laughing, he said, "Andy it is," as he whirled me across the dance floor. He was a wonderful dancer and managed to avoid anyone thinking of cutting in.

By the time the evening was over, he had asked my religion, my birth date, my political party, where I was from, how many sisters and brothers I had, and how long I had been in the Service. I had never before been grilled by someone I had just met. I thought to myself, "This guy is sure nosy," so I asked him the same questions. He was Catholic, I was Protestant. He was a Democrat and I was a Republican. How could any relationship develop here?

Looking at his arm patch, I saw he was a Specialist (A) first class. "What is a Specialist A?" I asked. "I am not familiar with that rate."

WHAT WOULD YOUR FATHER SAY?

"Specialist A stands for Athletic Specialist. They gave me that rate because I have a degree in Physical Education. I was one of the lucky ones. I lettered in four sports in high school and my coach was able to get me a full four-year scholarship to the University of Maryland. I had just started my third year when Pearl Harbor was attacked. My friends and I applied for deferments until we could graduate. The government approved the deferments as long as we stayed active in ROTC, attended school year-round and kept our grades up. I was able to get my degree before enlisting."

"Did you continue sports in college?" I asked, looking into those smiling blue eyes again.

"I played baseball, football and boxed."

"You boxed?" (I mentally added that to the Catholic and Democrat list.) I wondered if that was why his nose was crooked.

"I'll have you know, I was the Light-Heavyweight Intercollegiate Boxing Champion of the Southern Conference in 1941. My senior year in college, I helped coach boxing. My favorite sport, though, was baseball. I was a catcher."

"Did you go directly from college into the Navy?"

"I wanted to. There was a Recruiting Officer who came to speak with those of us who had majored in Physical Education. The Navy was starting the Athletic Specialist department and needed officers. I was told I would go in as a Commander if I signed up then.

"I rushed over to the Armory to tell the officer in charge that I had been offered a commission in the Navy and I wanted to accept it. I thought he was going to have a stroke. His face turned beet red and he shouted at me,

'WHAT DO YOU MEAN YOU WANT TO JOIN THE NAVY?
'YOU CAN'T JOIN THE NAVY, YOU ARE IN THE ARMY!!!'

"Unfortunately, I didn't check to see if he was right. I had signed so many papers to be able to finish school, I couldn't remember what I had signed. My friends who did check are officers in the Navy now.

"When I graduated from the University, I was sent to Fort Benning, Georgia, to Officers Candidate School. I hated the Army, and fortunately I washed out."

"You washed out? What did you do that caused you to wash out?"

He grinned, "Well, it could have been the time I was hurrying across the grounds, going to gas-mask training. My Captain fell in step beside me and asked, 'Mr. Gunther, where are you going?'

"'Gas-mask Training, Sir.'

"'Mr. Gunther, where is your gas mask?' I had forgotten my gas mask."

"More likely though, it was the time we were practicing firing mortars with live ammunition. My captain was a slow learner, and he put me in charge. We had to set up, sight and fire on command. When I gave the order to fire the first burst, there was this loud bang. I saw the shot take off, not where it was supposed to go, but straight up. I said to myself, what goes up comes down and I got the hell out of there."

I was laughing so hard, I couldn't dance.

"They sent me home to wait to be drafted. I got a job in a Defense Plant and waited for a while, but all my friends were serving and I couldn't stand waiting. I went home and told my

Mother, 'Mom, I am going down and enlist in the Navy. If they try to put me in the Army, I'm going over the hill. I don't want the Army.'"

"I was sure that with all my ROTC training, they would send me to the Army, but I lucked out. I ended up in Boot Camp at Great Lakes in Illinois. From there I was sent to Sand Point Naval Air Station at Bremerton, Washington. There, along with keeping the Airmen in shape, I coached and played baseball and I coached boxing. All the members of my baseball team were either pro or semi-pro players, including Freddie Hutchinson. It was a great experience."

I was impressed.

"It was great duty, but I wanted to do what I was trained for, rehabilitation of the wounded. I had been there about a year and I asked for a transfer. They sent me here. I thought I would be working with wounded veterans, but they assigned me to Unit III, the rheumatic fever patients. There isn't much they are able to do, mainly stretching and breathing exercises. Not what I had expected, but they are a great bunch of guys."

We danced until the band stopped playing and the hall started emptying out. Herb walked me to the WAVES Quarters where a group of my friends were standing, discussing plans for the next day. I introduced them to Herb. Vi's date, Kenny Hickel, looked at Herb's sleeve and asked, "Hey Herb, what does that 'A' stand for, America only?" Everyone, including Herb, laughed.

"I hope so," he answered.

Vi and Kenny

Roy Nilmeier spoke up. "Herb, we are all going to meet after lunch tomorrow and go bowling. Why don't you and Andy join us?"

"I'm game." Looking at me he said, "I'll bet you a steak dinner I can beat you."

"You must be out of your mind. You just got through telling me what a great athlete you are and you think I would bet you. I will go bowling, but I won't bet you."

Laughing, Herb said, "It's a date, then. See you at the Chow Hall at noon." With this, we all said goodnight and the fellows headed down the hill to their barracks.

CHAPTER 17

Never Bet with a Pro

S unday morning, I went to church at the base Chapel where I sang in the choir. After the service, Vi, Kenny and Roy were waiting for me outside. We walked up the hill to the Chow Hall. Herb was there, waiting. His face lit up when he saw me coming. This was the first time I had seen him in daylight. He was built like a Greek god, all muscle and bone.

Herb Gunther

Our friends were already in line when we entered the dining room. After lunch we headed for the bowling alleys. Herb chose a ball, turned to me, grinning, and asked, "Sure you don't want to bet a steak dinner?"

"No way!"

We started bowling. I was doing pretty well and I noticed that on Herb's first two turns, he got a spare and a gutter ball, then 8 pins and a gutter ball. Feeling more confident, I asked, "Do you still want to bet that steak dinner?"

"You're on," he said, smiling, as he picked up his ball and proceeded to throw strike after strike. I had been set up. When we finished bowling, we all walked back to the WAVES Quarters together. Everyone was laughing and teasing me.

Herb said, "I believe you have liberty tomorrow night. How about my collecting on our bet then? What time should I pick you up?" We set a time, 5:30 in front of my quarters.

As Vi and I started up the steps, I looked back. He was still standing there, smiling. I said to myself, "He is laughing at the way he suckered me. I hope I have enough money to pay for a steak dinner." When I got to our room, I checked. I had $15 to last me until the next pay day.

I expressed my concern to Vi and she said, "Don't worry about it, he won't let you pay for his dinner." She didn't know Herb Gunther.

It was New Year's Day, but a work day for me. After work, I hurried home, showered and slipped into my wool uniform, coat, hat, gloves and shoulder purse. I couldn't help worrying about having enough money to pay for two dinners and having anything left.

Hurrying down the wide rounding stairs, I checked out at the desk and out the front door. There he stood at the foot of the stairs, smiling up at me.

He took my arm as we headed down the hill to the gate. Showing our IDs, we were allowed to pass through the gate where we joined a group of Service men and WAVES waiting for someone to give us a ride. We didn't have to wait long. One of the patients I knew stopped, picked us up, drove us to Riverside, and dropped us off in the center of town.

"Do you have a preference or do you want me to pick a place to eat?" I asked.

"Since you are buying, you pick the spot. I actually haven't been here long enough to get acquainted with eating places."

"The Mission Inn has good food and dancing. We will go there. It isn't far from here."

I was pleasantly surprised. We each had a steak dinner and I had money left. After dinner, we went into the Ballroom where there was a big band playing. We danced until the band folded up for the night. I had had a wonderful evening.

When we got back to the base, Herb walked me up the hill. Stopping under a Eucalyptus tree across from the WAVES Quarters, he took me in his arms and kissed me goodnight. When our lips parted, he made a hissing sound through his teeth like steak on a hot griddle. My heart was beating like a drum.

"What are you doing Wednesday? Do you want to do dinner and dancing again?" he asked as he walked me to the steps. Smiling, he said, "I'll buy this time."

"I would like to, but Vi, Kenny and some of the gang from my office are going out. Would you like to join us?" His smile answered for him.

"Same time, same place, then," I said as I ran up the steps. When I got to the top of the steps, I turned. He hadn't moved. I liked this guy.

First thing Tuesday morning, I went next door and asked my friend Alice Glasser, who worked in the Personnel Office, if she would do me a favor. "Would you please check the records on Herb Gunther. He is 25, educated, an athlete, handsome, and he says he is single. This guy is too good to be true. I can't believe he could still be single." She agreed.

When we reached the Chow Hall, there he was, waiting for me. From then on, we met for every meal, and on my duty weekends we took advantage of the recreational things available on the base.

Alice called me at my office before noon and said, "It is hard to believe, but he is single." My heart skipped a beat.

Wednesday, Vi and I checked out and found Herb and Kenny were waiting for us at the foot of the stairs. As agreed, we met the rest of our gang at the Chicken Shack near Riverside. Best chicken west of my mother's kitchen.

We had been told there was a great blind pianist playing at a piano bar. He was amazing. We listened for awhile, but the place was so crowded and the smoke so thick, I suggested we leave. Vi, Kenny, Herb and I headed for the Ballroom at the Mission Inn. The music was great and we danced until they closed.

On the way back to the base, we told Herb of our plans to go to L.A. for the weekend and invited him to come along.

Friday, after work, we caught the train to L.A. Vi had made reservations at the Hayward, and Kenny and Herb found a room at the Roslyn Hotel. Since Herb had never been to L.A., we headed for the Studio Club in Hollywood and got tickets for special radio and stage shows for Saturday. We had dinner and ended up at the Palladium. We danced until we had to leave to catch the last street car back to our hotels.

Sunday morning, after breakfast, we showed Herb around L.A. until it was time to catch the train home. When we were settled in our seats, Herb asked to take me out on Tuesday, my next liberty night. "I hope you don't have other plans for that night," he whispered.

"I would love to go out with you Tuesday. No, I have no other plans." I laughed as it dawned on me that since we met, we had eaten every meal together and had spent every liberty together. Evenings after work on my duty days, if I hadn't been called to admit patients or special a patient, we were together. We hiked up to Jenson's Peak, went boating on the lake, or bowling with my friends. The only time we were not together was when I was on duty or on Sunday mornings: he went to Catholic services and I went to Protestant services; however, we had only been out as a couple one time, and that was to pay a debt.

CHAPTER 18

Could This Be Mr. Right?

At 5:30 Tuesday evening, Herb was waiting in the WAVES lounge when I came down the stairs. He took me to the Mission Inn again. By the time we headed home, I think we knew everything there was to know about each other.

We caught a ride to the hospital, and Herb walked me up the hill to my quarters. When we reached the top of the hill, we stopped under our Eucalyptus tree. Herb took me in his arms, kissed me and said, "I love you. Will you marry me?"

"What?" I thought I had misunderstood.

He held me close, smiling down at me as he repeated his question. "Will you marry me?"

"Marry you? You don't even know me. It hasn't been two weeks since we met."

"I know you. You were born Nov. 22, 1919. You have seven sisters and four brothers. You are from Indiana." He repeated everything I had told him that first night while we were dancing.

"Remember the night we met?" he asked. "I was in Ship's Service when you came in with Vi. I was sitting on the other side of the room, watching you, and you never even looked my way. You were too busy talking and laughing with your friends. When

I saw you smile, I said to myself, 'I am going to marry that girl'. When you got up to leave, I didn't even know where you were going, but I wanted a chance to meet you, so I followed you down to the dance. When you stopped off, I waited inside the door until you came in. I didn't want to give anyone else a chance to ask you to dance."

"So that is why you asked so many questions that night. I had to qualify." My head was spinning. "How did you know I wasn't married or engaged?"

"That never occurred to me. How did you know I wasn't married?"

"I had Alice check. I don't take chances," I said laughing.

"YOU CHECKED ON ME? You didn't believe me? You must have cared or you wouldn't have checked on me, right?"

"Well, I couldn't believe that a guy like you hadn't been nabbed by some girl, and I don't date married men. Like I said, I don't take chances." We were both laughing.

"How about you?" he asked, "You must have had proposals before. How have you managed to remain single? You must have been waiting for me."

"Yes, I have had proposals from men whom I had dated for months, not days, but I never accepted any of them. I have been waiting for Mr. Right. Maybe you are he? I don't know yet. I like you very much, but I need more time. Don't make me answer you tonight. I have to be sure." I was so taken by surprise, I didn't know what to think. I knew I didn't want to lose him.

Could this be Mr. Right?

He smiled at me and said, "I can wait as long as there is a chance." We kissed goodnight and I ran up the stairs to my room. I slept very little that night. Questions were whirling around in my head. I had never dated anyone whom I liked as much as Herb, but was I in love with him? There were so many questions. What about his church? Does love conquer all?

The next morning, I confided in Vi. "He is a great guy, Andy. Your concerns about his religion are justified, however. He will never marry out of his church, and to marry a Catholic, you must sign papers to raise your children Catholic. Can you do that?"

"I have thought about that and I don't think I could. I wouldn't object to being married by a Priest, but I can't make a promise to God that I know I can't keep. I didn't give him an answer. We have a date for Thursday and I will have to ask him about that. I really like him, but I have known him for such a short time, I don't know if it is Like or Love."

Vi hugged me and said, "Talk with him about it. Maybe you are borrowing trouble." We headed for the Chow Hall. Herb and Kenny were there waiting for us.

Thursday, I met Herb and, as usual, we ended up at the Mission Inn. When we got back to the base, we stopped under the Eucalyptus tree. He held me close and asked, "Am I Mr. Right?"

"I want you to be, but there are so many problems."

"What problems? Don't you think your family will like me?" he asked, smiling down at me.

"I know they would love you. That isn't the problem. You said you had been an altar boy since you were a child and all through college and you said you would never marry out of your church. I descend from generations of Presbyterian ministers. I don't object to being married by a Priest if I don't have to sign papers to raise my children Catholic. If they some day chose to become Catholic, I would never object, but I can't make a promise to God that I know I can't keep. My church makes no such demands on you. Why should your church make demands on me? Can you check with the Priest and see if that is the only way we can be married?"

Herb jumped up and clicked his heels together and then grabbed me again. "Did you just say you would marry me?" He was swinging me in a circle.

"I said I want to marry you if we can solve our problems."

"I will go to the Priest tomorrow and check with him. I am going to marry you!" He walked me over to my quarters, kissed me again and said, "I am going to marry you!" I watched him from the top step. He headed down the hill and I saw him jump up and click his heels again. I said a silent prayer that he would find a Priest that would give him the right answer.

When I reached my room, Vi was still awake. I told her everything. She hugged me and said, "I hope it works out. He is a great guy."

Friday morning, as Vi and I walked out of our quarters, Herb and Kenny were waiting at the foot of the steps to go to the Chow Hall. We ate breakfast and lunch together as usual. Herb had an appointment with the Priest in the afternoon and was not at the Chow Hall when Vi, Kenny, and I arrived. It was after dark when I was called to the phone. It was Herb; he asked me to meet him under our tree.

I rushed down, out the door, and there he stood, waiting. When I saw his face, I knew it was bad news. His smile was gone. "You talked to the Priest? What did he say?" I asked.

Herb looked at me with tears welling in his eyes, "He said you are a temptation put before me by God and I must give you up."

I couldn't believe my ears. "What did he say when you asked him what happens to the temptation if she signs the papers?"

"I didn't think of that," he said. Holding me close, he buried his head in my hair and said softly, "If I can't marry you, I don't think we should see each other again. I love you too much." He kissed my cheek, turned quickly and headed down the hill.

As I watched him go, I wanted to call him back, but what would I say? I had never felt such emptiness. I went up to my room. Vi and Edie were out. I was glad to be alone to think. I tried to catch up on my letters to Wayne, Mom, Grandpa and my sisters and brothers at home. All the time, I kept asking myself, "Should I have agreed to sign the papers?" But I knew that would have been dishonest and unfair to Herb.

The next morning, I told Vi everything. "Do you think I am an idiot? I am sure now he is Mr. Right, and I let him walk away."

Vi took my arm and said, "Come on, let's go to breakfast. I'll bet he is there waiting."

When we reached the Chow Hall, there Kenny stood by himself.

It was my liberty weekend, but I stayed on base, hoping for a call. It didn't come. I didn't see Herb all day Saturday or Sunday. Sunday evening around nine, I had just gotten into my pajamas and robe when I was called to the desk. I had a phone call.

When I picked up the phone, I was so happy to hear Herb's voice on the line. "Would you like to take a walk, he asked?"

"Give me ten minutes. I'll meet you outside." I took the steps up to my room two at a time, changed back into my uniform, grabbed my coat, ran down the stairs and out the door.

There he stood at the foot of the steps. His smile was back. He led me into the shadows and held me close. "I couldn't stay away," he said. "I went on liberty with some of the guys Saturday night and today, but it was no fun. I knew I couldn't be on the same base with you and not be able to be with you. I had to see you."

"What about the Priest?" I asked.

He was still holding me in his arms. He looked at me and said, "If I ask you to marry me again, it will be your way. You know I am Mr. Right, don't you?"

I kissed him and said, "Yes, I believe you are." We were back where we had been. Life went on as if nothing had happened. Nothing was mentioned about marriage.

Most of the time, we double-dated with Vi and Kenny. They had a wonderful relationship. They both had a great sense of humor. Vi was from El Paso, with that soft Texas drawl. We would crack up just listening to her talk. She had very straight hair and got regular tight permanents. Kenny affectionately called her Mop Head and she called him an Old Goat. Kenny kept asking her to marry him and she insisted she was too old for him.

CHAPTER 19

Snowbound

I had liberty the weekend of March 2, 3 and 4. Vi and Kenny had planned on visiting Vi's cousin in Burbank that weekend. Rita, Alice and their boyfriends had reserved a cabin at Big Bear Lake. They invited Herb and me to join them. Alice's boyfriend offered to drive his car.

As soon as we got off work Friday, the six of us piled into the car, headed to Redlands and up the mountain. The road was narrow and twisty. When we got about halfway up, it started snowing heavily, making visibility difficult.

It was late when we reached Big Bear, found our cabin and checked in. The cabin had a small kitchen and two bedrooms, each with a double bed, and a large closed-in front porch that acted as the living room. We dropped off our luggage and went searching for a place to eat nearby. The wind was now gusting, piling snow up on the sides of buildings and burying parked cars.

After dinner, we headed back to the cabin and turned in. I hadn't slept three-in-a-bed since I was a little girl, but we were so tired and tense from the scary ride up the mountain, that we slept. We didn't ask how the guys managed.

When we stepped outside the next morning, it was a winter wonderland. Snow had fallen all night. Cars in the parking lots were covered with new snow and it was still snowing and blowing. Huge icicles hung like swords from the edge of the cabin roof, waiting to drop. The sun shining on all that snow was blinding.

Big Bear

We found a café, had breakfast and then wandered around the quaint little village, in and out of shops, ending up at a grocery store where we picked up snacks for lunch, salads and steaks to barbeque for our dinner, and returned to our cabin. It was still snowing. Our driver was worried. He constantly checked the weather and road conditions on his car radio.

After dinner, Herb and I decided to go for a walk while our friends stayed in the warm cabin, playing cards. It had stopped snowing. The moonlight on the snow seemed to create a carpet of diamonds as it lit our path. It was a clear night and the sky was filled with stars. They seemed much closer to earth here than down the mountain.

Walking was difficult in the new snow, but we made it down to the lake. We stood there, our arms around each other, and watched the moonlight dancing on the frozen lake. Suddenly, Herb turned me to face him. Holding me close, he smiled down at me and said, "Will you marry me?"

This guy was an expert at shock treatment. I looked at him, studying his face in the moonlight. I wanted so much to say yes, regardless of conditions, but I said, "How about your Temptation?"

"I told you if I asked you again, it would be your way. If that is the only way you will have me, we will be married out of my church. I love you and I want to spend the rest of my life with you."

As we clung to each other, I said, "I love you, too, and I want to marry you, but are you sure that the time won't come when you will resent me for this decision? I feel terrible that either of us has to make such a choice. How about your family? Will they accept me?"

"I didn't ask you to marry my family. I asked you to marry me," he said, smiling. "They will love you. I have thought it through. I believe the way we met was no coincidence. We were meant for each other and I know God will bless our marriage regardless of who performs the ceremony."

"I feel the same way. I think I knew you were Mr. Right the first time you proposed. I was so afraid you wouldn't ask me again. I love you so much and I will be proud to be your wife."

It was snowing heavily again as we stood there embracing, oblivious of the cold. We promised each other that we would not let anything or anyone get in the way of our love for each other as long as we lived. I had never felt so filled with joy and happiness.

Herb looked down at me with those smiling blue eyes and said, "Let's get married right away."

I pushed back and asked, "Would you mind having a formal wedding? I have always wanted a formal church wedding and I would like Vi to be my Maid of Honor. Just running off to a Justice of the Peace, I don't think I would feel married."

"I figured we would get married right away, but if you want a formal wedding, we will have one," he said, smiling at me. "How long will it take to arrange it, a month?"

"Not so fast. There are a lot of things we have to do.

"I have to ask the Captain for permission to marry you and for permission to wear a wedding gown. We have to go to L.A. to get a marriage license. We have to have blood tests. We have to choose a church and reserve it. How about June?"

"JUNE? That's three months from now."

I laughed at his impatience and said, "You have things to do, too. I don't have a ring."

He smiled sheepishly and said, "I didn't know what size you wore and thought we would go together to pick them out. Besides, what if you had said no? I doubt that they give you a 30-day return guarantee. I would have been stuck with a ring and would have had to look for someone it would fit." We both laughed.

"We had better get back to the cabin. This snow is really coming down. Let's not tell the others of our decision to marry, I want to tell Vi and Kenny and Rose and Vern before we tell others." Herb agreed.

We headed back to the cabin. The snow had filled in the path. I was holding onto Herb's arm and wading through drifts. He had snow boots but I didn't. By the time we reached the cabin, my feet were wet and cold.

Everyone had gone to bed. Rita and Alice were already asleep. I slipped into bed beside Rita. I was so happy and excited, but my head was so full of questions and misgivings that sleep evaded me until exhaustion took over. Even with all of Herb's assurances, I couldn't help wondering, "Am I doing the right thing? Will the time come when he will regret this decision?"

Sunday morning, when we awoke, it was still snowing. It had snowed all night. We decided to walk to the village for breakfast. The sun on the snow-covered landscape was blinding. Joe checked the weather report. There had been a snow slide blocking the road to Redlands. Barring other slides, they hoped to have it cleared by 1:00 p.m. Joe was worried. He and his friend had to be back at their base before midnight or they would be AWOL. I was more worried about his drinking and thinking of his driving those dangerous roads down the mountain with five passengers in the car.

Big Bear cabin and our car

One o'clock came, but the slide had not been cleared. They thought it might be cleared by three.

We started checking to see if there was another way out. One of the old-timers told us of an old logging road down the back side of the mountain, through the desert, Twenty-Nine Palms, around the mountain to Banning and Beaumont and then on to Corona. This was a dangerous road even in good weather.

At three, the road still was closed. Our car had been packed for hours and we decided we couldn't wait any longer. We headed east, found the logging trail and started down the mountain. It was a slow, twisting ride and it was snowing again. It was dark before we reached the desert floor and got onto level ground. When we did, we all breathed a sigh of relief. The wipers were doing a poor job keeping the snow cleared from the windshield.

It was still snowing, but Joe could see the road ahead and he picked up speed. Suddenly, out of nowhere, a calf dashed in front of the car. Joe swerved, trying to avoid it, but we felt a thump as the car sideswiped it.

Joe's comment was "I'll bet he has a headache in the morning." He didn't even slow down. It snowed until we got out of Beaumont and almost to Redlands. Snowplows had been working and we were all relieved to see clear roads.

We reached the hospital about ten. I was never so glad to get back to the base. Herb helped me out of the car and as we headed up the hill to my quarters, he whispered, "I have never in my life been so glad to get out of a car. I was saying Hail Mary's all the way down that mountain."

I laughed and said, "With three Catholics and a Protestant all on the line to God at the same time from the same car, how could He not listen?"

CHAPTER 20

Spreading the News

I ran upstairs to my room. Edie was still out, but Vi had just gotten in.

I set my suitcase on my bed and burst out, "Vi, will you be my Maid of Honor?"

Vi looked at me and her face lit up, "He did it! He asked you again?"

I was beaming with joy. "Yes, he did. I am so happy, but I am scared."

Vi rushed across the room and hugged me. "I can't wait to be your Maid of Honor. Why are you scared? You know he loves you and you love him."

"I know that, but we are being married out of his church. I am so afraid the time will come that he will regret that. I feel guilty that he is giving up his church for me."

Vi hugged me and said, "Don't borrow trouble. It was his choice and he made it. Now we have to plan that wedding. I couldn't be happier for you."

Monday morning, as Vi and I stepped out of the WAVE Quarters, we saw Herb and Kenny coming up the hill to meet us. They were both smiling.

Kenny gave me a hug and said, "Herb tells me you finally asked him to marry you." He laughed as he ducked the swat I aimed at him, and added, "I couldn't be happier for both of you."

After breakfast, Herb and I went to my office, where I introduced him to my boss, Mr. Anderson, and the civilian ladies who worked in the office. The guys already knew him; they had bowled with him the first weekend we met. I then announced that we were being married in June. The office exploded with congratulations and well-wishes. Everyone was excited and happy for us. Herb went on to his ward in Unit 3, and our office went back to work.

The two civilian ladies who worked in our office volunteered to help us in any way they could. One told me of a print shop nearby where we could get our invitations made. Another told me of a small rental that was becoming available. "The owner only rents it to help out Service people. Places are so hard to find. I don't know what they are asking, but I am sure it is reasonable," she said.

Monday, Herb and I spent the evening writing our parents, families and friends. My first letter was to Wayne. His year of overseas duty was almost up and I wanted him to be at my wedding.

Tuesday, we went to check out the print shop my friends had told us about. The owner was a real help. We went home with a large book of wedding announcements and invitations from which to choose.

The rental was another story. It was an old chicken house that had been converted to a one-bedroom apartment with a small bath, a hot plate and a sink. The wall separating the tiny living room from the tiny bedroom was an old metal Coca-Cola sign, its bright lettering not even painted over. Someone must have scavenged it from a roadside billboard. This is what they do to help poor desperate Service men??? We had three months and it wasn't difficult to pass up that "bargain."

Vern told us of a jeweler we could trust, and invited us to come to their home for the weekend. "I will take you over to his place. I have known him for years and I know he will give you a good deal."

My next weekend liberty, Vern picked us up and drove us to L.A. We stopped at the jewelers on the way to his home. After picking out my rings, we were told we could pick them up in two weeks.

Rose was still at work when we got to their home. I called her and asked if she had plans for dinner. She said she had a rabbit in the refrigerator. I started preparing dinner.

"Herb, have you ever eaten rabbit?" I asked.

"Rabbit! You have to be kidding. I would never eat rabbit."

Vern winked at me as he said, "Herb, while Ruth fixes dinner, let's go down to the corner bar. I want to introduce you to some of my friends."

By the time Rose got home, dinner was ready. She gave me a hug and said, "Ruth, you can't imagine how nice it is to come home and not have to cook. Thank you so much. I am anxious to meet that lucky man you have chosen. You know Vern and I are so happy for you."

Just then, Herb and Vern came in. Rose rushed up to Herb, gave him a big hug and, smiling, she said. "You must be Herb. I hope you know how lucky you are to get Ruth. She did tell you that you have to pass our inspection, didn't she? Vern and I couldn't be happier for the two of you. I want to wish you both all the happiness in the world. Now you men go get cleaned up before Ruth's dinner gets cold."

By the time Herb and Vern came back, Rose and I had dinner on the table. As we were eating, Herb said, "Ruth, this is the best chicken I have ever eaten."

"Well, thank you, Herb, I am glad you like it."

Vern couldn't hold it. "Do you know what you are eating, Herb?"

"Sure, it's chicken," he said, as he looked up and saw all of us smiling. "Rabbit?? It tastes like chicken," he laughed with us.

CHAPTER 21

Wedding Plans

On my duty nights, unless there were patients to admit, Herb and I spent the evening in the WAVES Lounge, going through the book from the printers, picking out our wedding invitations and announcements and making lists of those we wanted to invite to our wedding.

I went to the WAVE officer in charge and asked her to arrange a meeting with Captain Jenson so I could get permission to marry. I also had to have permission for my bridesmaids and me to wear gowns. Service personnel were not allowed to wear civilian clothes at any time during wartime without permission from the Captain. She set up the appointment for the following week.

The day of the appointment, I went to Lieutenant Rombold's office and accompanied her to the Captain's office. His Secretary said, "The Captain is expecting you. You may go on in."

Entering the Captain's Office, we saluted and stood at attention. Standing, Captain Jensen returned our salute. As he looked at the papers in front of him, he asked, "Lieutenant, is this the young lady who wants to get married?"

"Yes Sir, may I present Corpsman 2/C, Winona Anderson. She has asked to see you to request permission to be married."

I stood there at attention, frightened to death. "Miss Anderson, who do you want to marry?"

"Herbert Gunther, Sir."

"Is he in the Service?"

"Yes Sir, he is in the Navy."

"What is his Rate?"

"He is a Specialist A1/c, Sir."

Captain Jenson looked at me sternly, and raising his voice, he asked, "A Specialist A! Miss Anderson, couldn't you find a good Corpsman?" He then smiled broadly and said, "You have my permission and I hope you will be very happy. Is there anything else?"

"Yes, Sir, I would like to have a formal wedding and would like your permission for my bridesmaids and myself to wear gowns."

"You have my permission and best wishes," he said, smiling. I am sure he heard my sigh of relief as we left the office.

I asked Rita and Alice to be my bridesmaids, and they excitedly accepted.

Vern West was to give me away. Everything was falling into place so perfectly.

Vi's Cousin, Marie, and her husband, Ernie Nicholson, had invited us to have our reception in their yard in Burbank. They told Vi and Kenny to bring us to their house for the weekend to check it out.

On our next liberty weekend, Friday the 30th of March, we took the train to L.A. and caught a streetcar to Burbank. We loved the yard and Marie's idea of lighting it with Chinese lanterns.

The next morning, we sent the guys off to entertain themselves while Marie, Vi and I went into L.A. to J. W. Robinson Co. to shop for gowns.

While I was trying on wedding gowns, Vi picked out a beautiful pastel for her Maid-of-Honor gown. I ended up with the first gown I tried on, a cream colored, corded taffeta with a sweetheart neckline and a long flowing train. We all agreed it was perfect. Marie suggested that we leave our gowns at her house until the wedding. Vi and I would stay there the night before the wedding. Herb and Kenny would stay with Vern and Rose.

Now we needed to find a wedding chapel. Marie suggested that we check out Forest Lawn Memorial Park. Herb and I had been granted a two-day pass for Monday and Tuesday so we could get our license and reserve the chapel. Marie insisted we stay there the two extra nights.

Sunday, April 1, 1945, we took a street car to Glendale and found the Memorial Park. What a beautiful place. Herb looked around, put his arm around me and, smiling, said, "I am glad there are no headstones. My friends will never believe I was married in a cemetery."

There were three churches to choose from. The first one we entered was the Church of the Recessional. We had gone in the wrong door and found ourselves in the Crematorium. Herb grabbed my arm and said, "Let's get out of here. I could never be married in this church." We left laughing.

The next church we found was The Wee Kirk o' the Heather, an exact replica of Annie Laurie's church in Glencairn, Scotland. With my Scottish ancestry, that sounded right to me. We went into the church. It was beautiful. It was just the right size with a seating capacity of 85. On the left side of the church was a flower aisle looking out into a garden of flowers.

Wee Kirk of the Heather

Outside, to the left of the church, in a beautiful garden, was a wedding chair where couples sat for pictures. There was also a kneeling bench. Herb took my hand and drew me down beside him. As we knelt there, we asked God to bless our marriage.

We didn't have to look further. We knew this was the right church for our wedding. As it was Sunday, there was no one there to help us. We would have to go back on Monday to speak with someone about reserving the church.

Monday morning, we went to the jewelers and picked up my rings. They were perfect. From there we went back to the church. We were able to reserve it for June 10, 1945, and were given stacks of paper to read before meeting with the Wedding Coordinator the next morning.

Tuesday morning, we went back to the church and made a deposit of $25.00 ($10 for the assistant's fee, $5.00 for the organist, and $10 for the deluxe wedding). The deluxe wedding not only included a white satin floor runner and kneeling bench, but also a large bell that hung above the altar where the bride and groom stood. When the minister said, "You may now kiss the bride," the bell would open, showering the couple with rose petals.

From the church we went to the Courthouse in L.A. to get our Marriage License. We got in just before closing time. The lady behind the desk filled out the license and said, "That will be $2.00 please."

I stood watching as Herb pulled out his wallet, opened it and pulled out a five-dollar bill. He handed it to the clerk, who said, "I am sorry, sir, but it is late and I have no one-dollar bills left. You will have to have exact change."

Herb turned to me and with a sheepish grin asked, "Can you loan me two dollars?" We left the Court House laughing and headed back to the base.

I reminded Herb years later that he never did pay back that loan.

CHAPTER 22

The Best Laid Plans

S ervice women had not been allowed to serve in combat areas. In late 1944, the government determined that Hawaii was now safe enough to allow women to serve there on a volunteer basis, thus relieving men for the battlefront.

Vi and I immediately volunteered. I had told Herb about this, but with all the excitement of planning our wedding, I hadn't thought about it since.

One evening, we were sitting in the WAVES Lounge, working on our wedding plans, when Herb asked, "Andy, you told me you had signed up to go to Hawaii. Have you withdrawn your name from the list?"

I gasped, "Oh my! I hadn't even thought about it. I had completely forgotten about it."

"Don't you think you should?" he asked.

"I will do it first thing in the morning. What if my orders had come in? I can't believe I forgot that."

First thing after breakfast, I rushed up to the Personnel Office and checked. No orders had come in, so I was allowed to withdraw my name. I was so relieved; I could hardly wait until lunch to tell Herb. I had no idea how lucky I was until I got back to my quarters that evening and saw Vi. She was standing there with a handful of papers, waiting for me.

"Andy, I got my orders this afternoon. If you hadn't removed your name from the list this morning, you would be going, too. I am happy for you that you will be able to be married, but sad I won't be here for your wedding. I was looking forward to this transfer, but I wanted so much to be your Maid of Honor," she said. As we hugged each other, neither of us could hold back the tears. I was happy for Vi, but I knew how I would miss her and so wanted her for my Maid of Honor.

"When do you have to leave? I know we were all going to the Inn dancing tonight, but would you rather spend your time with Kenny alone? If you would, you know Herb and I will understand."

Smiling she said, "No, this is my last night. I want to spend it with my friends. I get five days leave and then I have to report to Long Beach for shipping out. I am going to spend those five days with Ernie and Marie. Kenny has been given a three-day pass and will join us while I am there. I am excited and sad at the same time. I am excited about going to Hawaii, but sad that you can't transfer with me and I am leaving all of my friends behind. How many of my friends will I ever see again? When the war ends, I will be in Hawaii and they will scatter all over the country to pick up their lives where they left off."

I gave her a hug and said, "Enough of the sad stuff. You will never get rid of Herb and me. Let's go celebrate. Kenny and Herb will be here any minute."

We had a wonderful evening, and Vi left early the next morning. Now I had to find someone to be my Maid of Honor.

When I got to my office, Vern was waiting for me with tears in his eyes. "Andy, I am not going to be able to give you away at your wedding. I just got my orders to report to Long Beach Naval Hospital for Duty. I am so sorry." I gave him a hug as I fought back tears.

"You and Rose will be at our wedding, won't you? You two are my family out here."

Smiling through tears he said, "If I am in the country, we will be there. You know we wouldn't miss your special day."

Everything had been going so perfectly until now. I began to have misgivings. Was God trying to tell me something?

We went ahead with our wedding plans. I mailed out the invitations and I chose another friend, Carol Smith, to be my Maid of Honor. I asked Austin Horn to give me away. Herb asked Roy Nilmeier to be his Best Man and Kenny Hickel and Gus Mueller to Usher. Floyd Hinman's, eight-year-old daughter, Virginia, was thrilled when I asked her to be my flower girl. Tony Giacobbi talked his eight-year-old son, Anthony Jr., into being our ring bearer. Our friend, Joe Puccio, agreed to sing. I began to relax. Everything was falling into place so beautifully. Herb asked, "Who will we get to perform the ceremony?"

"If you don't mind, I would like to ask Lieutenant Wickham, the Protestant Chaplain here on the base. I have attended his services and sung in his choir ever since I got here, so I know him well. It is a lot to ask of him to drive to Glendale but I think he will do it. Is that okay with you?" I asked.

Herb smiled at me and said, "You know him and like him. That is fine with me."

After church, I waited until everyone had filed out. Chaplain Wickham was standing at the door. I asked, "May I speak to you, Sir?

"Certainly, Winona, how can I help you? Is everything okay?" he asked.

"Oh yes, everything is fine. I have met a wonderful man and we are going to be married in The Wee Kirk O' The Heather at Forest Lawn Memorial Park. I wanted to ask you if you would consider going to Glendale to perform the ceremony."

He smiled, "I would be delighted. May I bring my wife?"

"You certainly may, but first, I have to ask you something. In the service, do you ask the bride to obey her husband or to love, honor, and cherish him?"

His smile broadened as he responded. "I say, love, honor, and cherish."

"You can marry us, then," I said, laughing with him. "I do have a more serious concern though." I proceeded to tell him about Herb choosing between me and the Catholic Church. I told him the whole story and about my fears that someday he would regret it.

Chaplain Wickham smiled and said. "He must love you very much to have agreed to marry you out of the church. Love is a very powerful thing, but it takes a lot of giving on both sides to keep it going. Don't expect that if you go halfway you will have a 50/50 marriage. If you both strive to give 100%, trust in God and each other, you will make it and have a wonderful life together. Check with Herb and pick a day when you can both come in to see me before the wedding. Just give me a call and I will put you on the calendar."

I felt reassured, "I will talk with Herb and call you. Thank you so much," I said as I turned to leave.

I rushed up the hill to meet Herb at the Chow Hall. Just before I got there, I heard someone calling my name. Turning, I saw the Chief in charge of Ship's Service hurrying toward me.

"Andy, there is an apartment opening up on the second floor of the building in which my wife and I live. It is yours if you want it. I already talked to the landlord and recommended you. I have received my orders and will be shipping out, and I would feel better knowing you and Herb lived there, since my wife and her mother will be living by themselves in the apartment downstairs. I don't want the landlord to pick just anybody. He understands and has agreed to let us pick the new tenant. The place is a mess, but it is a nice one-bedroom apartment if you don't mind cleaning and painting at your expense. You will have to pay for the month of May even though you won't be living there. It will take a month to get it ready to move in. My wife has the key, and if you like it, it is yours."

"That is wonderful. I don't know how to thank you, Chief. Herb and I have liberty tomorrow. We will be there as soon as we can get to Corona. Thank you so much. I know my friends from the office will help us get it into shape."

When I reached the Chow Hall, Herb was standing there with Kenny. "Hey, guess what? We have an apartment." I proceeded to tell them everything the Chief had said. "Do you want to go with us to see it tomorrow, Kenny?"

Herb answered for Kenny. "Sure he does. He is going to be in charge of the work crew."

Kenny laughed and agreed. "You can count on me. I would love to see it. I have to write and tell Vi what it is like."

"Oh! I forgot to tell you, Herb, Chaplain Wickham agreed to marry us, but we have to pick a time to meet with him. I think everything has been taken care of, now that we have an apartment. Maybe we can relax and spend our nights and weekends off, cleaning and painting."

CHAPTER 23

The Best-Laid Plans May Not be the Best Plans

April 12, all flags were at half-mast. We heard on the radio that President Roosevelt had died and Vice President Harry Truman was now President. All the commentators were talking about the fact that President Roosevelt always picked weak Vice Presidents and didn't keep them informed about what was going on in government or the war. Whether you liked Roosevelt or not, we were in the middle of a war and one could not help being anxious, not knowing what to expect.

Monday, April 23rd, Herb, Kenny and I headed for Corona. We found the triplex on Seventh Street and knocked on the door. Mrs. Nelson answered our knock and said "Hi, you must be Andy. My husband said you were coming to see the apartment. Let me get the key and you can go on up and check it out. It needs a lot of cleaning. If you go up these stairs, the apartment is the one on your right. The landlord does nothing except collect the rent. It is a nice apartment, though. Which of you young men is Herb?"

Herb stepped forward, extended his hand and said, "I am Herb and our friend here is Kenny Hickel. He just got drafted to be head of our work crew. We will check out the apartment and bring this key right back. I am sure we will take it regardless of the shape it is in. We really appreciate the Chief recommending us. We promise to be good neighbors, and if we can do anything to help you after your husband leaves, just yell up the stairs."

Running up the stairs, we unlocked the door and stepped into a large living room furnished with an old couch, two chairs and a couple of small tables. On the east wall were two large, double-hung windows looking out toward town. I wondered how long it had been since they had been washed.

Through the living room at the front of the house, we entered a nice-size bedroom that opened onto a small balcony. It was sparsely furnished with twin beds and an old chest of drawers.

Back through the living room to the back of the apartment, we walked into the kitchen. Thank goodness, we had been warned. To the left of the door was a small gas range. I was sure it was white, but so dirty it was hard to tell. It was covered with what must have been years of baked-on food that I hoped could be removed. That would be my first project. A small, filthy, GE refrigerator with its circle of coils on top stood at the right of the door. The kitchen sink and a bank of cabinets covered the west wall. A door in the corner of the north wall opened onto a nice little screened-in porch which looked out onto the backyard. There were a small table and two chairs on the porch. Inside the kitchen, at the right of the door, was a large window under which stood a table and two chairs. The window would allow cross-ventilation and could be used as a pass-through to the porch.

We knew we would have to scrub every inch of the place before we could paint or anything else, but we loved it. It sure beat the chicken house with its Coca-Cola sign partition, and the rent was the same.

Kenny said, "I think it will be fun helping you two clean this place up. While you guys go sign papers, I am going over to Cap's Place to have a beer with the guys. Maybe I can do a little recruiting while I am there. See you back at the base."

Mrs. Nelson told us where we could find the landlord. "He is expecting you," she said, smiling. We found his house, were interviewed, signed a rental agreement, paid our rent and got two sets of keys. We were ecstatically happy as we headed back to catch the last bus to the base.

I rushed up the stairs to my room and found Alice and Rita waiting for me. Before I could tell them my great news, Alice said, "Andy, we can't be your bridesmaids. We asked the Priest for permission and he said you are sending Herb to hell if you marry him out of the church, and he won't let us participate."

I was in shock, hurt and angry. We had been friends for so long, I couldn't believe what I had just heard. "You knew when I asked you that we were being married out of the church. You must have known that you were required to get permission. Why didn't you see the Priest before you agreed to be my bridesmaids?"

Alice spoke for both of them. "Well, we hadn't expected the Priest to refuse us permission." I looked at her and she knew I saw through her. This was calculated. They hoped to stop our marriage.

As they started to leave, Rita turned and said, "I am sorry. Andy. I had looked forward to being your bridesmaid." I could see in her face that Rita felt bad about what they had done.

I wanted to call Herb to meet me under our tree, but decided I would wait until morning to tell him. I wondered if the Priest had told him I was sending him to hell.

I was still in shock and deeply hurt. I went next door and told my friend, Betti Peterson, what Rita and Alice had done. "I had asked them because they were my first friends here. It never occurred to me that the church would forbid them to participate."

"I know, Andy," she said. "Alice and Rita were here earlier and told my Catholic roommates that she and Rita were backing out. I couldn't believe it."

"I know it doesn't give you much time to shop for a gown, Betti, but would you consider being my bridesmaid?"

"I would love to be your bridesmaid. I was hoping you would ask me to fill in. I can hardly wait. This will be so much fun," she said as she hugged me. "I will get together with you before the weekend and find out what I need to know."

As tired as I was, I had trouble sleeping. Strangely, most of my friends were Catholic. I felt sure Alice had passed the word around among the other Catholic girls. Would I have to choose a bridesmaid based on their religion? I hadn't picked my friends that way and it wasn't the way I wanted to live.

The next morning, while I was getting ready to go to work, my friend Nan Varese, came into my room. She said, "Andy, I heard that Alice and Rita decided not to stand up with you. I am Catholic, but I think what they did is unforgivable. If you haven't chosen anyone else, I would consider it an honor to be your bridesmaid."

Hugging her I said, "Oh Nan, I wanted to ask you, but knowing you were Catholic, I didn't want to put you in the position of having to refuse, I think God sent you to me. Thank you so much, I feel better about Catholics now and I know it will mean a lot to Herb. You can't imagine what a weight you have lifted off my shoulders. You know, Nan, I am glad Rita and Alice backed out. Now I know I have real friends standing with me.

"By the way, Herb and I found an apartment yesterday and we signed the lease. It is a mess but most of the guys from the office have volunteered to help clean and paint. Wednesday, we are going to eat on base and then catch the bus to town. We will make it a party every night we are off and would love to have you join us whenever you like."

"That sounds like fun. I'll do it. I am off Wednesday," she said excitedly. "How about cleaning supplies?"

"The guys in Supply have that taken care of." I answered. "Herb is off tonight. I gave him a list and he has gone shopping for rubber gloves, steel wool, razor blades and a bunch of other stuff. We will be close enough to stores, we can pick up anything I forgot."

"Great, I will meet you here Wednesday after chow, with some old clothes ready to go. I am so excited," she said as she gave me a hug and left.

I grabbed my purse and hurried down the stairs and out the front door. Herb was waiting for me at the foot of the steps. He asked. "Are you okay? You look tired."

"I am fine. I didn't sleep too well." As we walked up the hill to the Chow Hall, I told him what had happened, leaving out the part about my sending him to hell.

"Rita and Alice were waiting for me when I got home last night. They told me the Priest had refused to allow them to be my bridesmaids. I didn't know they had to have permission. Wouldn't you think they would have asked permission before they accepted?" I asked.

Herb put his arm across my shoulder and hugged me to him. "Don't worry about them. I am sure you will find someone else."

"Oh, I already have. Nan Varese, one of my other Catholic friends, came up to the room this morning. She had heard that Alice and Rita had backed out. She said, 'I am Catholic, but if you haven't chosen anyone else, I would consider it an honor to be your bridesmaid.' Betti Peterson from next door was excited when I asked her."

Herb smiled down at me and said, "I like both of them. I think you made great picks. I am so glad Nan offered. Alice and Rita will see their little sabotage job didn't work."

CHAPTER 24

The War In Germany Ends

We figured we had fourteen evenings and three weekends to get the apartment cleaned and supplied. Tuesday was my duty night, so Herb went shopping for the things on my list. He got a case of beer, some soft drinks and snacks for our workers.

On Wednesday after Chow, Nan, Herb and I met Kenny at the gate with his work crew. All the guys from the Property and Equipment offices, that didn't have a wife living near the base, had volunteered. Austin Horn, with his dry Southern accent and wit, kept everyone laughing. They worked, laughed, and joked until it was time to catch the last bus back to the base. Kenny with his crew showed up every night we had liberty. The crew thinned out on the weekend, but Kenny, Roy and Austin showed up faithfully.

I took my radio to the apartment to follow the news on the war in Germany. Things were happening so fast in Europe now. On Saturday, April 28, they announced that the Italian Partisans had hung Mussolini. Our apartment exploded with cheers. The following day, the American Army liberated the Dachau concentration camp. We all felt that if the war in Germany would end, the U.S. would concentrate more on Japan and the war would end.

I hadn't heard from Wayne for some time. I knew he was in combat somewhere around Manila, but didn't know where. He had received my letter about my upcoming marriage and had written, wishing me happiness. He said, "I should be back in the States in May sometime and hope to be able to get leave to attend your wedding. My year overseas is almost up."

We were called on more often now to admit patients. Since we were short of Corpsmen, our short work day had been extended from eight hours to nine and a half hours. The long day remained the same. We went an hour earlier and got off at 5:30.

After a nine-and-a-half-hour day in the office, an order came out that all available Corpsmen were to report topside to admit patients. Rushing through dinner, we reported as ordered. Herb, not being a Corpsman, went to work in the apartment.

In the past, most of our patients had been shipped from the battlefield to Long Beach or San Diego, and the ambulatory patients were then transferred to Corona. Many of these boys looked as if they had come directly from the front. They were ambulatory or in wheelchairs, but many were in bad shape. We worked as fast as we could to get them to their assigned wards.

One man had a groove where his eyes had been. He was a very tall, handsome man in his late twenties. I introduced myself and asked, "Would you like to take my arm? I took his hand and placed it on my arm. Realizing it was an uncomfortable position, I added, "Since you are so much taller than I, perhaps you would feel more comfortable holding onto my shoulder."

As we walked to his ward, his hand gripping my shoulder, I talked to him about the things that were available at the hospital, particularly the swimming pools and the dancing.

He listened politely and then said, "They tell me Corona has the best doctors of any of the Navy hospitals. Do you think they will be able to help me?"

I was glad he couldn't see the tears roll down my cheeks as I answered. "We do have great doctors here. If anything can be done to help you, you are in the right place." We were at his ward, where another Corpsman took over. Before I left, I took his hand and said, "God bless you, I will pray for you."

He held onto my hand and said, "Thank you, Andy. I hope I will see you again."

Wiping the tears from my eyes, I said a prayer for this young man as I hurried back for my next patient. It was after 0200 when I deposited my last patient and headed back to my quarters. I couldn't get the sight of those mangled bodies out of my head; however, I was so exhausted, I must have fallen asleep the minute my head hit the pillow, and I dreamed.

I was on the battlefield in my Corpsman uniform. In the distance I saw a group of fifteen or twenty soldiers digging in. Among them was my brother Wayne; his red hair shone in the moonlight. I started to run to him when I saw a Japanese soldier crawling toward the dugout. He stopped, raised up, and I saw the grenade in his hand. Pulling the pin on the grenade, he drew back to throw it. I screamed, "Wayne!!" but it was too late. The grenade had landed in the middle of the dugout.

When the dust settled, there were three soldiers standing, two redheads and a dark-haired young man. I ran to them. Wayne had his back to me. "Wayne, Wayne!" I said, but he didn't turn. I took his arm and turned him. His face was a mass of bloody flesh, not recognizable. I awakened, sitting up in a cold sweat, shaking like a leaf. It was so real, I got up and wrote the time on my calendar. I spent most of what was left of the night praying for my brother until sheer exhaustion took over.

The alarm went off at 0600, and as I dressed for work, I remembered the dream. I reasoned that this horrible dream was caused by seeing and hearing the stories of the patients I had just admitted.

Herb and Kenny were waiting for me when I walked out the door. Herb took my arm, and as we walked up the hill to the Chow Hall, he asked, "Have you heard that Hitler committed suicide? I just heard it on the radio." After hearing Herb's news, I forgot about the dream.

"No, I hadn't heard. Praise God! Hopefully, that means in a matter of days the war will be over in Germany and all those men in prison camps will be released. Your brother Charles should be coming home soon, and those like your brother, Walter, who have been fighting for months, may be sent home. That is great news.

"Isn't it a strange feeling?" I added. "The war is over on one side of the world, but we are still fighting Japan on the other side of the world, a completely different kind of war with a people of a completely different culture, who swear they will fight to the last man. I hope Truman will send more help our way."

I had mixed feelings. I rejoiced in the defeat of Germany, knowing so many families would be reunited, knowing they could once again go back to normal, peaceful living; and I grieved for those who would have no one coming home, but my brother was fighting in Manila. The war wasn't over for him or for the thousands of other young men scattered on islands all over the Pacific.

May 2nd, German Troops in Italy surrendered, and on the 7th there was the Unconditional Surrender of all Troops. The war in Germany was over. Everyone rejoiced and they were sure Japan could not hold out forever. We went on with our lives as usual.

By Saturday, I had my refrigerator and stove cleaned. I left the guys cleaning the kitchen ceiling and walls for painting while I went shopping for paint at Corona Hardware at 120-122 E. Sixth Street. I bought the paint and wandered through the hardware looking for things I needed for my kitchen. There was very little in cookware to choose from. No factories were making pots and pans. I had already bought a coffee percolator and a thin, one-quart aluminum pan.

I put a $10.00 deposit on a 53 piece dinner set, a teakettle, 2 kitchen forks, a set of mixing bowls, a water set, apron, and nest of cast-iron skillets (six- and eight-inch skillets and Dutch oven with a glass lid). The total came to $29.30 including seventy-one cents tax, and the salesman, Chuck, delivered it all to the apartment. I felt I could manage with these things. Each payday, I made a payment until this bill was paid off.

The fellows in supply had picked out some Navy-surveyed single sheets, a couple of blankets with cigarette burn holes in them, and silverware for our table. The silver had worn off, but the "USN" was plainly visible. We joked about our mono-grammed silver.

I again went to Corona hardware and, on credit, I purchased a little eleven-pound Singer sewing machine for $99. I also bought the folding table that was made to hold it. We moved the twin beds together, and using the worst worn sheets to patch the others, I sewed them together to fit the bed. (I think I invented the king-size bed, but never got credit for it.) I repeated this with our surveyed blankets, burn-holes and all, with USN showing proudly.

CHAPTER 25

The Dreaded Letter Is Delivered

May 14, 1945, I was sitting at my desk when Rita came in with the mail. I thought she had a concerned look on her face as she handed me my mail, but when I recognized Wayne's handwriting on the first letter, I hurriedly opened it without even glancing at the return address. The first sentence hit me like a bolt of lightning.

> Well, your little brother finally got one hung on him. I am in an Army hospital in San Francisco, but I am fine, so don't worry about me. Maybe I will get to come to your wedding, after all.

> You always told me to keep my head down, but it didn't work this time. I took some shrapnel in my jaw, taking out some teeth and a piece of the jaw bone. As a result, my mouth is wired shut and I am eating liquid food. They have to let the swelling go down before they can operate to do a bone

graft. It will be months before they can fit me with a partial plate, but I don't mind. Ground food beats C-rations any day. I just thank God I am one of the lucky ones. I came back.

We had been in heavy combat and had killed or scared off most of the enemy. We were cleaning out pockets of stragglers in the mountains around Manila. The officers had hired some local Philippine men to work for us in camp. When we noticed they had disappeared, we started digging in. We had worked with Freedom Fighters: they loved the Americans and fought right along side of us. These workers were different: they would work for whoever paid them the most. When they disappeared, we decided we had better take cover. There were twenty of us digging in for the night when a mortar shell dropped in on us. I guess God isn't through with me.

Since we were constantly getting replacements for the many men killed or wounded, we no longer knew who all was in our company. The Medic who found me was a friend of mine from Wolcott, Indiana, Vernon Spear (we always called him Pud). Neither of us knew anyone else from our home area was in our Company. He told me later, "If I hadn't seen that red hair, I would have passed you up for dead. Your face was a bloody mess and covered with flies. I said to myself, 'That looks like Pinky Anderson,' and I went over to put a wet handkerchief on your face to keep the flies off. When I found you were breathing I stopped the first soldier who passed. He happened to be a friend of ours from Indiana. Fortunately he had type A-positive blood, so I plugged you in. You are one lucky guy, Pinky." Pud had given me a transfusion from our friend right there on the field. I owe them my life.

Unbelievable, isn't it? I was given a transfusion on the field, by a friend, from a friend, along with a welcome shot of morphine. I never thought God would send Angels in uniform, but he did.

Pud asked, "Pinky, can you walk?"

He had pumped me so full of morphine, I said, "Hell, Pud, I can fly."

As I read Wayne's letter, I couldn't believe it: He was describing my dream. My heart was beating rapidly and my hands shook as I turned the pages. God had answered my prayers that night. I was thanking God as I continued to read.

A Catholic Chaplain came by and said, "I don't know what your faith is, Pinky, but it doesn't matter." He gave me the Last Rites.

They carried me over the mountain to a dock where I waited with other patients until we could be loaded onto a Hospital Ship. By this time, my tongue was so swollen I could scarcely breathe, let alone talk. The Medics had inserted tubes to help me breathe. Another Priest was passing through the rows of wounded, praying for everyone. When he got to me, he gave me the Last Rites again. When I got on board ship, the only thing that worried me was getting seasick with my mouth swollen shut. Drowning in my own vomit was not the way I wanted to go. I sure was glad when we finally got to San Francisco and I felt the ground beneath my feet.

I wasn't aware that the whole office staff was anxiously watching me until I turned to tell them the good news. With tears threatening to roll down my cheeks, I said, "My brother has been wounded, but he is going to be okay. He is in an Army Hospital in San Francisco, awaiting corrective surgery. He was hit in the jaw by shrapnel that took out some bone and teeth. They have wired his jaw shut and are waiting for the swelling to go down so they can operate to do a bone graft."

My office exploded with cheers of joy for me. I knew they had been praying for Wayne. What a great gang of friends.

I had a hard time getting down to work. I read and reread that letter to see if I had missed anything. At noon, I rushed out to the Chow Hall to meet Herb and tell him my good news. I felt so relieved for myself, but sad for Herb. I knew he had been anxiously waiting for news of his brother Charles. His family had had no news from Charles since they were told he was captured in Italy by the Germans and was a prisoner of war. It had been eighteen months with no news. His brother Walter was with Patton's Third Army, and Herb had heard nothing from him for weeks.

When I told Herb my news, he grabbed me and swung me in a circle. "I knew he was going to make it," he said, beaming down at me.

After Chow, Herb headed for the apartment to paint and I went to my room to answer Wayne's letter.

After telling him how happy I was that he was back in the States, I told him in detail about my dream. I wrote,

> When I read your letter, I couldn't believe it. It was so like my dream: it was as if I had actually been on the battlefield with you that night. And to have two of your friends from home just happen to be there at that time to find you. You are right: God sent Angels in uniform to save you and they didn't even know they were angels. God answered my prayers that night, little brother. I am so sorry you had to come home this way, but I am glad you are out of the fighting. I hope you can make my wedding, but I will be surprised if your doctors give you leave until they fix you up. I will understand if you can't make it.

We had Tuesday and Thursday off and spent our time working at the apartment. Friday morning, as Herb and I were climbing the hill to the Chow Hall, he said, "You know, I told you, we First-Class guys in our department never checked out or in when we went on liberty. We knew we were supposed to, but no one ever checked on us, so we never bothered. Well, apparently they decided to start checking and didn't mention it until after the fact. I have an invitation to meet with the Captain today."

"Isn't that invitation called Captain's Mast?" I asked. "You guys have gotten away with murder. Because you have a first-class rate, you have your own quarters, and you told me the lower-rate guys clean your barracks for you. WAVES don't get away with that: rate only means more responsibility and a little more pay. I'll bet after your invitational meeting with the Captain, you will be restricted to the base."

Herb laughed, put his arm across my shoulders and squeezed. "I promise, I will not forget to check out again."

As expected, Herb was restricted to the base for Friday through Sunday. Fortunately, that was my duty weekend, so we didn't mind. Our crew had almost finished the painting. We still had three evenings and a weekend in May to finish the restoration job on the apartment, unless Herb had another Invitation from the Captain.

CHAPTER 26

Our Rehearsal Dinner

Sunday, our last weekend liberty before the wedding, we invited all our cleaning crew for a home-cooked dinner to celebrate the completion of the restoration project. Since our wedding party was basically our cleaning crew, this would also be our rehearsal dinner.

We spent Saturday buying last-minute things for the apartment and groceries for our party. I had found a small grocery store with a good meat market not far from the apartment. People gave the owner their extra stamps to be used to help Service people who weren't issued stamps. While we were working on the apartment, Herb and I had become friends of the butcher. I had bought lunchmeat and a couple pork chops once in a while and he never asked for stamps, but I had never asked for anything large. This time I was serving twelve people.

I went into his store and said, "Chuck, Herb and I, with the help of our friends, have finished cleaning and painting our apartment. We have invited our whole cleaning crew over for dinner Sunday to celebrate. I know I am asking a lot but do you have anything I can buy, without stamps, to serve twelve people?"

He smiled and asked, "How about a nice roast? I have one that needs to be used by tomorrow." I wanted to kiss him. I bought what I needed for the dinner and went back to the apartment. Herb had just finished washing the windows.

While I put things away, Herb ran downstairs and borrowed a couple of card tables with chairs from Mrs. Nelson, and a table and chairs from the girls across the hall. We covered the tables with our Surveyed Navy tablecloths, and set them with my new dishes, glasses, paper napkins and our "USN" monogrammed silver. They were beautiful.

Sunday morning, after church, we stopped at the Chow Hall for lunch and then caught the bus to Corona. As soon as I got in the apartment, I started preparing for our guests. I made pie crust from a recipe on the Crisco can. The chopping block/counter next to my stove would work fine for a pie board. Suddenly it dawned on me: I hadn't bought a rolling pin. I ran across the hall to see if our neighbors had one: two working girls, they had no use for a rolling pin. I noticed a wine bottle in their trash and asked, "May I have that? I can clean it and it should work fine." I headed back to my kitchen, bottle in hand, problem solved. I had bought one can of Comstock apple pie filling and one of cherry. Soon the aroma of baking pies filled the apartment.

Herb borrowed an ice chest from Mrs. Nelson, set it on the porch off the kitchen and filled it with an assortment of canned drinks. While I was making my pies, he went to the store and brought back a bag of crushed ice and poured it over the drinks.

While the pies baked, I prepared the roast in my new cast-iron Dutch oven. As soon as the pies were done, I set them on the table to cool and put the roast in the oven. While I made a huge salad, I put Herb to work scrubbing potatoes for baking. I placed the potatoes in the oven beside the roast and put the salad in the refrigerator.

Herb was eyeing the pies. Turning to me he said smiling, "Don't you think these pies need to be tested to be sure they are good enough to serve?"

I gently pushed him out of the kitchen as I jokingly threatened, "You touch those pies and I will break your arm."

"You wouldn't do that. I wouldn't be able to put the ring on your finger."

"To keep you out of trouble, why don't we go for a walk?" I suggested, "We have an hour and a half before I need to do anything here."

It was good to get out of that hot kitchen for a while. We walked to the park and through the rose garden. The roses were in full bloom and the fragrance was breathtaking. We sat down on a bench and enjoyed them.

Herb said, "You should see my mother's roses. We live in a row-house. The backyard is very small, but it is full of roses. Every time one of us boys gives Mom roses for a special occasion, she puts one in the ground in her garden, puts a canning jar over it and it grows. When the huckster men come down the alley with their horse-drawn wagons, she takes her coal shovel out, picks up the horse droppings and puts them in her rose garden. She has the prettiest roses in Baltimore."

I looked at him to see if he was pulling my leg. "I am serious. Just wait until we go back there and you see her roses."

"I can't believe they have horse-drawn hucksters. When I was little and lived on the farm in Indiana, our huckster men drove trucks. I live in a small town of 3500 people and you never see horses on the street anymore. I was in New York and I didn't see any hucksters."

"In Baltimore, everyone lives in row houses. The streets are very narrow. The alleys behind the houses are even narrower than the streets. Horses work better than trucks." I was anxious to see this strange town. I would love to see the hucksters with their horses and wagons.

We continued our walk and took the long way back to the apartment. Before we opened the door, we could smell that wonderful aroma of roast beef and fresh-baked pie. My roast and potatoes were done. I turned the oven off, transferred the roast to the iron skillet and set it back in the oven to keep warm while I made gravy from the drippings, dressed the salad, fixed the coffee and set it on the back burner, ready to turn on when the time came.

Having caught the bus together, our guests all arrived at the same time. They had stopped at the store on their way and were well supplied with beer, wine and snacks. When they arrived, they wandered through the apartment, admiring their work and our finishing touches. They were proud of their part in creating what now looked like a home.

Our rehearsal dinner was a huge success. The girls helped me with the dishes and the guys returned the borrowed tables and chairs before they left. I took what little food there was left across the hall to our grateful neighbors. We locked up the apartment and left for the last time before our wedding and caught the last bus back to the base.

Monday morning, Kenny and Herb were waiting for me in front of my quarters. They were both laughing. "What is so funny?" I asked.

Herb grinned sheepishly and said, "Well, you know how I promised I would be sure to check out from now on? I kept my promise: I checked out, but I forgot to check back in, so as far as the Navy was concerned, I was AWOL. They seem to be a little touchy about that, so I got another invitation from my friend, the Captain."

I couldn't believe my ears. I said, "Herb Gunther, you are going to mess around and be restricted to the base the weekend of our wedding." He and Kenny were still laughing.

Herb put his arm around me and, smiling, said, "Don't worry, I will not be restricted the weekend of our wedding, I promise. I will only get three days restriction and we have finished work on the apartment. You have duty two of those nights and we agreed we need to save our money for the wedding, so we can't afford to go out anyway." I shook my head and laughed with them.

CHAPTER 27

One More Stumbling Block

*I*t was Monday, May 28, 1945. Leaving Herb and Kenny at the Chow Hall, I reported to work and told the office crew about Herb being restricted to the base again. Austin Horn said, "Andy, that guy is going to mess around and miss his own wedding." Everyone laughed.

Mrs. Fortner, one of the civilian ladies spoke up, "Andy, if he is restricted, I will put him in the trunk of my car and take him out with me, so don't worry." We were all laughing.

"The way things have been going, I may have to take you up on that. I think he has learned his lesson, though.

When I met Herb for lunch, he had a broad smile on his face. As we went into the Chow Hall he said, "I decided to accept the Captain's Invitation, but he didn't give me a three-day restriction. He is such a generous guy, he gave me a whole week. We weren't going out anyway, were we?" Those smiling blue eyes were so disarming.

We made use of the time on the base. We climbed to the top of the hill everyone called Jensen's Mountain, where you could see for miles. We signed out a rowboat and I taught my city boy how to row. He was a fast learner once he got the hang of it, but by that time I was well sprinkled. We wrote thank-you notes. The nights when the gang was on base, we went bowling, but by this time I had learned not to bet with the Pro.

Time passed quickly. Our rehearsal was Wednesday June 6th. Kenny, Joe Puccio, Herb and I rode with Roy Nilmeier, who had volunteered to take his car. There were enough people with cars that we were able to get rides for the whole wedding party to and from Glendale. Joe and Kenny arrived together. It was obvious that Joe had been drinking. I took his arm and whispered, "Joe I don't care how much you drink after the wedding, but please don't drink before the wedding."

Joe laughed, put his arm around my shoulders and said, "Andy, don't you worry about me. I will be cold sober at your wedding."

The rehearsal went beautifully. Kenny and Joe took off to make the most of what was left of their liberty night while the rest of us returned to base.

Thursday was a Duty day. Everyone had made their plans for rides to L.A. on Friday. Vern West had invited all the guys in the wedding party to his house for a bachelor party. I would be in Burbank at Ernie's and Marie's home, preparing for the reception.

Friday morning, Herb met me for breakfast. His smile was gone. "What is the matter?" I asked. "You don't look happy this morning."

He shook his head, "Do you remember me telling you they never had Captain's Inspection in our quarters? Well, that suddenly changed. They had inspection this morning and our quarters are restricted for the weekend. They had never inspected our quarters before. We have a new officer in charge and I guess he is trying to make us feel like we are in the Navy. Maybe you should ask Mrs. Fortner if she was serious when she offered to take me out in her trunk."

I couldn't believe my ears: one more obstacle. You can't change a wedding date two days before the wedding. We hurried through breakfast and then to my office to tell our friends. There had been so many things tripping us up along the way as we planned our wedding, I couldn't help thinking, was God trying to tell us something? Maybe he didn't want Herb to marry out of his church.

When we walked in, Austin Horn looked up and said, "Hi, Herb, any more invitations from the Captain?"

Herb laughed and said, "This one wasn't an invitation. It was more like a command performance. I think you jinxed me, Horn, when you predicted I would be restricted to the base on my wedding day." The laughter ceased, followed by dead silence.

As Herb explained what had happened, everyone groaned. Mrs. Fortner came over, put an arm around me, and, looking at Herb, she said, "No one is going to stop this marriage. Herb, you have someone else take your luggage for you. We don't want to draw any attention when I put you in the trunk of my car. We can leave with the rest of the civilians. Be at the back of the building at 5:10. I will drive my car around and you can slip into the trunk. I will drop you off outside the gate wherever Roy tells us to meet him."

I gave her a hug and Herb gave her a kiss on the cheek. "You are an angel," he said. "I will be here on time. I can't thank you enough. I'd better run. I don't want to get in trouble for being late to work."

Promptly at 1700, we all gathered at the door of the supply office. It was not unusual for a bunch of us to be in that office after hours. There was someone on duty in that building at all times, guarding the supplies.

We often gathered there, visiting with the civilian ladies before they left. Or, on duty nights, if we weren't called to special a patient or admit patients, our gang would frequently hang out there, just visiting. We had a hot plate, a coffee pot and refrigerator for our use. This is where I often fried the fish the gang caught. The large doors opening to the loading dock gave us plenty of fresh air to keep the smell of fried fish out of the office area.

Mrs. Fortner took her time getting her car. She pulled up to the door after the other workers had driven away. Our friends thoroughly enjoying shutting Herb in the trunk while I dashed back to my quarters for my coat and luggage.

Roy was waiting in front of the WAVE Quarters when I came down. Taking my things and placing them the trunk, he said, "Everything went off okay. I saw Mrs. Fortner go through the gate as I was driving up here. She is going to let Herb out at the first crossroad. We shouldn't be far behind them. Herb put his gear in my trunk last night."

Sure enough, when we reached the first crossroad, Herb stepped out from behind a tree, smiling at us.

Roy dropped me off at Marie's home in Burbank, and he and Herb continued to Vern's. I learned later that the guys kept Herb up all night.

Marie and Ernie had strung Chinese lanterns around the yard, and Ernie had set up a long picnic table at one edge. Saturday morning, Marie and I went out shopping for things needed for the reception.

Herb and I had previously ordered our wedding cake, a tiered cake with a sailor and bride standing in the center of the top tier. It was ready when Marie and I stopped at the bakery to pick it up. It was perfect.

I spent Saturday afternoon and most of Sunday preparing for the reception. Sunday morning, Marie gathered enough roses from her garden to fill two crystal vases. After covering the table with a beautiful linen tablecloth, she placed a vase of roses at each end. By the time we finished, it was time to leave for the church. The refrigerator was filled with little sandwiches and fruit punch. After the wedding, Marie would have everything out by the time the bridal party arrived.

CHAPTER 28

The Most Beautiful Wedding Ever

Mr. and Mrs. Gunther

Ernie pulled the car out of the garage and Marie helped me hang my dress in the backseat. I climbed in beside it and we drove to the church. Ernie waited outside while Marie walked with me. We followed the wedding coordinator around the side of the church and into the bride's room in the back corner of the building. After getting us settled, she returned to the front of the church to see that everything was going as planned.

Marie helped me into my gown with its yards and yards of corded taffeta. After making sure the veil was properly set so it would fall softly over my face as well as down over my shoulders, she left to join Ernie.

My bridesmaids arrived soon after I had dressed. They were beautiful in their rainbow of soft pastel dresses of pink, yellow and green.

The wedding coordinator stepped in and whispered, "It is time." She lined everyone up as they were to enter the church and gave the bridesmaids their flowers, cascades of sweet peas.

I had chosen to carry the small white Testament Aunt Winona had given me when I first joined the Service. I had left it with the coordinator, allowing time for the florist to attach to it an exquisite white Cattleya orchid with a dark pink-colored throat. It was gorgeous.

As we reached the entry to the bride's waiting room, off the vestibule, I could hear Joe's beautiful baritone singing "Because," followed by the "Kashmir Love Song." Suddenly I was startled by several loud blasts from the organ, followed by the Wedding March.

I watched as the bridesmaids, one by one, headed down the aisle, followed by my flower girl, eight-year-old Virginia Hinman, in her beautiful light-blue dress. She loved being a part of my wedding. Virginia carried a basket of rose petals which she dramatically tossed out on the white satin runner that covered the aisle from the rear of the church to the altar.

Austin Horn stepped up, smiling as he offered his arm. I was shaking like a leaf, and as we started walking, he whispered, "Andy, you are supposed to walk down the aisle, not dance." I pinched his arm.

We stood for a few seconds, facing the front of the church. It was full of mostly Navy personnel, a sea of blue and white. I saw my whole wedding party standing facing me. Our ring bearer, eight-year-old Anthony Giacobbi, looked so sharp in blue pants and a white coat, standing proudly, holding the white satin ring pillow.

The Chaplain and Best Man stood with Herb at the foot of the altar, but all I could see was Herb. He looked so handsome in his Navy Blues, standing there. His smile was radiant and his eyes never left me, making me feel like the most beautiful bride to ever walk down an aisle. I could feel my heart hammering. I had never before felt such joy. All my fears, misgivings, worries and doubts seemed to melt away. I knew at this moment that Herb Gunther was the man God had chosen for me. I was not making a mistake.

Austin and I started walking toward the front of the church. My long, full train filled the aisle behind us. When we came to the third pew, Herb stepped forward. His smile broadened when he could see through my veil. Taking my hand, he placed it on his arm and, turning, he led me to the white satin-covered kneeling

166

bench. We knelt as Chaplain E.H. Wickham asked God to bless this marriage, followed by Joe singing the Lord's Prayer.

The service was beautiful. After exchanging vows, "Promising to love, honor and cherish each other until death do us part," Herb placed the rings on my finger. When the minister said "You may now kiss the bride," Herb gently laid my veil back over my head and, as we kissed, a huge paper bell above us opened, showering red rose petals down upon us. There were soft sighs from the pews.

We turned, facing the full church. Reverend Wickham said, "I would like you to meet Mr. and Mrs. Herb Gunther."

Herb took my arm and we hurried up the aisle to the exit. Near the back of the church, I saw Rose and Vern sitting next to the aisle. Rose was beaming, but I saw tears running down Vern's cheeks. I smiled at them and, reaching down, I gently laid my hand on his cheek. In return, I received a loving smile from both of them as Herb hurried me out.

Bride and Groom

It seemed that everyone had a camera. The Forest Lawn photographer took so many poses of us and the bridal party, it seemed to take hours. I was worried no one would be at the reception to cut the cake. When we finally left the church and arrived at the Nicholson's, we found that Marie and Ernie had everything under control.

Herb and I stood behind the table, serving punch, sandwiches and wedding cake, laughing and joking with our guests. Joe Puccio stepped up across the table from me, knelt, and told me what a beautiful bride I was and that he loved singing at my wedding. I could tell he had had a few drinks, but he did not appear to have overdone it.

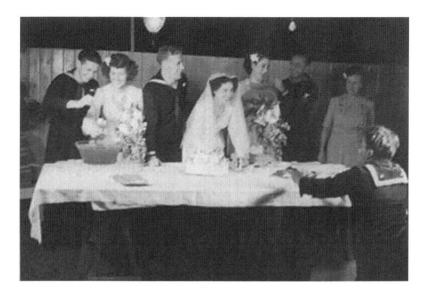

Wedding Reception

Leaning over the table, I thanked him and said. "Joe, your beautiful singing made the wedding. I love hearing you sing and I want to thank you for keeping your promise."

Laughing, he said, "Andy, you didn't doubt me, did you?"

The reception ended at ten. Our gang pitched in, helping Ernie and Marie carry things into the house before thanking them and leaving. Herb and I couldn't thank them enough as we hugged them and said our goodbyes.

Roy pulled his car up to the house and we climbed in. I was still in my gown. Marie and Ernie were still standing on the porch waving as we drove away. They had been wonderful to us.

I thought to myself that I must write to thank Vi for introducing us, and describe the wedding to her.

We hadn't gone far when we saw a crowd gathered around two sailors on a street corner. Roy slowed down and opened his window. We could hear that beautiful baritone: It was Joe singing while Kenny passed the hat, collecting from the appreciative audience. Laughing, Roy said, "That guy doesn't miss a beat even when he is drunk."

"Well, at least he waited until after the wedding to get drunk."

Herb and Roy laughed at my statement. Roy said, "You didn't see the guys helping him into the back of the church before the wedding, did you?"

Looking at them in shock, I said, "No I didn't. Was he drunk? I can't believe it. He didn't miss a note or word. Are you sure?"

They were both laughing and I remembered Joe kneeling in front of me, saying, "Andy, did you doubt me?" He didn't say he hadn't been drinking. I laughed with them and said, "Well I am glad I didn't know or I would have worried."

It must have been midnight when we got to our apartment. Roy ran ahead of us, deposited our luggage at the top of the stairs and left. Herb unlocked the door and carried his bride over the threshold. We were exhausted, but we agreed ours was the most beautiful wedding we had ever attended and the most wonderful day of our lives. Our wedding could not have been more perfect.

Monday morning, we caught the first bus from Corona to the hospital. It was necessary that we report in on time and then pick up the three-day pass which had already been granted. Walking through the gate, we showed our ID's and were waved on. We both heaved a sigh of relief. Herb apparently had not been reported as being AWOL.

When we stopped at the Chow Hall for breakfast, Herb's Chief came up, congratulated us and whispered, "You lucky stiff. The Officer of the Day knew you were being married and left word at the gate that if you tried, you were to be allowed through. How did you manage to slip out, anyway?"

Herb laughed, "I'll never tell. I might have to do it again someday. It is nice to know, though, that the Lieutenant has a heart. He is the guy that decided to inspect the barracks after all these months and restricted us for the weekend."

After breakfast, we picked up our passes and stopped by the Post Office for our mail. I had none, but there was a telegram waiting for Herb from his Brother Ed. Herb's hands shook as he opened and read it. I stood anxiously waiting. When he looked up, those blue eyes were swimming in unshed tears. "My brother Charles is home safe from the prison camp. Ed is sending a letter to give me more information. While you are getting what you need from your room, I am going down to my quarters to call Mom. I will meet you at your quarters after I talk to her."

After packing a few things in an overnight bag, I went outside to wait for Herb at the foot of the stairs. He was already hurrying up the hill, so I went to meet him.

He was beaming as he told me, "Mom is so happy, she could hardly talk. She had received a cable earlier, saying the camp where Charles had been held had been captured by the Russians. No one trusted the Russians. Nothing had been heard from him since. Some of the families of other prisoners of war had received cables that their boys were being returned, and several were already home. Mom was sure something had happened to him. She was out in the alley, talking to her friend Mrs. O'Brian, when she heard a familiar voice calling out, 'Hi Mom.' She looked up, and there was Charles, all smiles, rushing to lift her off her feet and swing her in a circle. Both were laughing and crying at the same time." (We would learn later that the cable arrived a week after Charles got home.)

Our joy was complete. Both of our brothers were back from the war and safe. We had a three-day pass, a full refrigerator, a deck of cards, $6.00 between us, and our rent was paid up to the first of July. What more did we need? This was our honeymoon.

Wedding Party

CHAPTER 29

Will My New In-Laws Like Me?

*E*arly Thursday morning, we caught the bus for the hospital and reported for duty. Everyone was happy to see me back at my desk. They raved about what a beautiful wedding we had had.

It was fun being back at work with my friends, but I was glad this was my short day. Tonight was our last liberty night until Monday. Since we were broke, we planned on spending it at home in our apartment. Except for our liberty weekends, we ate on base before going home. This allowed us to save money for the thirty-day leave we had requested. Those thirty days would be spent traveling back to Baltimore and Indiana to meet our respective in-laws.

Work was different now. It was a waiting game. Patients that could be discharged were sent home. Some of the Army bases were closing. On July 7th, a group of us were bussed 23 miles from Corona to Spadra. We were to take inventory of the Spadra Army Convalescent Hospital. This hospital had been taken over by the Navy and was being managed by our hospital. I don't know if it was because the Army no longer needed it or if we no longer had room for all the patients being admitted at Corona.

Our 30-day leave was approved starting Monday, August 6th. We had planned it to begin on the day after our weekend liberty, thus allowing us to slip in a couple extra days. After work on Friday, August 3rd, we caught a ride to San Bernardino and boarded the train to Baltimore.

The train was packed, standing room only. We ended up in an ancient Club Car, empty except for an old, overused oak bar. We were told they would be adding more cars at Flagstaff, Arizona. I guess the engine could only pull so many cars up that long grade. From there it was downhill. There were several Service men in the car with us, standing or sitting on the floor. Herb and I were the only ones behind the bar.

I had worked all day and was exhausted. Herb put an arm around me and said, "Andy, you look so tired, why don't you lay your coat on the floor and try to rest? I will sit here beside you."

I looked around. I was the only lady in the room, and looking back at my husband, I said doubtfully, "Are you sure it is all right?"

Grinning at me, he took his boxer's stance and said, "No one would dare touch you with the Champ here to protect you."

"Okay, but if we have children, don't you dare tell them their mother went to sleep on a barroom floor." We were both laughing as he spread my coat out, and I was happy to lie on it. When we reached Flagstaff, he had to awaken me.

On August 6th, we learned that President Truman had ordered the first atomic bomb to be dropped on Hiroshima. When we stopped in stations, we saw pictures on the front pages of all the newspapers.

I had heard from patients of the horrific things the Japanese had done to our boys and didn't think anything we did to end the war was too bad, but I still could not help but shudder as I read the description of the complete devastation it caused. Surely the Japanese would surrender now. We waited only three days, and our planes dropped a bomb on Nagasaki. Everyone was sure this would bring the Japanese to their knees.

The closer we came to Baltimore, the more anxious I became. "Herb, I have no idea what to expect when I meet your family. You have told me so little about them. Do you think they will like me?"

He thought for a minute and answered, "Well, don't expect my sisters to like you. I think my brothers will like you. You can kiss Mom, but I don't know about Pop." His answer did nothing to relieve my growing fear.

I asked, "Why do you think your sisters won't like me?"

With a little shrug, he answered, "Well, you are taking away their baby brother." I studied him for a few minutes. I still hadn't learned to know when he was serious.

We finally reached Baltimore. My ankles were swollen from sitting and sleeping in our seats for five days and six nights. I was so happy to finally get off the train into the huge Pennsylvania Station. We found cabs lined up at the curb, and Herb chose one, put our luggage in and told the driver to take us to 416 W. 25th Street. I was fascinated by the row houses lining both sides of the narrow streets, with their marble steps jutting out onto the sidewalk. The quaintness of the city with its ornate gas street lamps on every corner and horse-driven hucksters going up and down the narrow alleys, shouting, "Hard Crabs Alive," gave me the feeling of being in London in one of Charles Dickens' stories.

I was so fascinated by my strange surroundings that I was surprised when the taxi stopped at the corner of 25th Street. The street was on a high bluff overlooking the switching yard for the Baltimore and Ohio Railroad. The other side of the street was lined with row houses. The street was only one block long. Picking up our luggage, Herb led me down the sidewalk to the next-to-the-last house on the block. Smiling, he said to me, "This is my home."

Setting our luggage on the sidewalk, he took my arm and we climbed the steps. Before he could touch the knob, the door opened and before me stood a huge man. Laughing, Herb said, "Andy, this is Pop." Herb had told me his father was six-foot-five and weighed 250 lbs. That was no exaggeration. He was all of that. Pop was completely bald except for a ring of curly white hair around his head, just above his ears. He had the same laugh, strong voice and blue eyes as Herb. We stepped into a room full of Gunthers.

Suddenly I was lifted off my feet in a gentle bear hug. "I said I was going to give my new daughter-in-law a big hug," he said, as he planted a kiss on my cheek. I felt the heat rise in my face. I hated that I blushed so easily; however, all the tension over meeting Herb's family had disappeared. Everyone was laughing. Mom was smiling at the two of us as she gathered me in her arms and welcomed me into the family. She was no more than five feet tall. Her face was a picture of many years of love, joy, sorrow, worry and rejoicing. I instantly fell in love with her and Pop.

Anna was next in line, hardly able to restrain herself. She wanted to get to her little brother. Anna had a booming voice and a laugh to match. Herb had prepared me for Anna: He had told me that at one of his boxing matches, when the referee raised his hand in victory, he heard a booming voice from the highest balcony, shouting, "That's my baby brother!"

Anna was on us, "Herby Joe, I thought you would never get here," she said as she hugged and kissed him repeatedly. "We have your leave all planned out for you. Tomorrow Dorothy is having everyone over at her home so they can meet your new bride and you can see the rest of the family. Walter is out of the Service now and back at his old job. Dorothy's working, so she could not be here today. Stephen and Edward are working, but they will all be at Dorothy's tomorrow." Taking a breath, she turned to me, smiling, gave me a hug and said, "I hope we all don't scare you away. We get a little loud at times. I hope you and Herbert will be very happy."

Charles, with his rusty red hair, stood smiling his approval, waiting for a chance to get to Herb. What a joyful reunion. No words needed to be said: Herb was hugging the brother that he feared he would never see again. They were hugging and laughing and everyone was wiping away tears. Charles was a very bashful, quiet man, but he returned my hug and, looking at Herb, he said, "You did a good job picking a wife, Herb."

Herb put an arm around me and, laughing, said, "I think so."

Turning, he saw Mary, his oldest sister, waiting patiently. Mary favored her mother in looks. At the age of 16, she had run away to Virginia and married Donald Philbin, a young man from a very prominent and well-to-do family. In spite of their age, it

177

was a good marriage. His family loved Mary and moved her into their home. They treated her like a daughter. Her mother-in-law taught her how to entertain and to run the household as the wife of a prominent man should, but she never had a home of her own. Mary had been more like a second mom than a sister to Herb. Mom had not been well after Herb's birth, and Mary took care of him much of the time. She had a daughter six months younger than him, and the two had played together as children.

Mary hugged her baby brother as tears rolled down her cheeks. "Herbert, I am so glad to see you so happy." She turned to me, hugged me and said, "Andy, I can see how much Herb loves you and I am so happy to welcome you into our family. We want you to come over for dinner and meet Donald while you are here."

Herb had an arm around each of us as he promised his sister, "We wouldn't miss it, Mary. I have told Ruth what a good cook you are. Just pick a time and we will be there."

After a long visit, one by one the family scattered, leaving us with Mom. Putting an arm around her, Herb said, "Mom, Ruth and I haven't had much rest. We slept sitting up for six nights and are pretty bushed. I think we will try to get some rest before Dorothy gets home." Herb picked up our luggage and we climbed the stairs to his old room.

Herb went right to sleep. As tired as I was, I could not sleep, but I rested. After about half an hour, I heard the gate to the alley squeak and voices floated up to our room from the backyard. I nudged Herb and said, "I think your sister is here. Don't you think I should go down and offer to help your mother?"

Herb awakened, sat up and said, "Let's go down. I want to introduce you to Dorothy. You can offer to help my mom, but she won't let you."

Dorothy had been working and was still in her work clothes when she came through the back door. Although she was obviously tired, she lit up when she saw Herb waiting to greet her. Turning, he introduced us and Dorothy hugged me saying. "I am so sorry I wasn't here when you arrived, but I have to work. We have all been so anxious to meet you."

"Thank you, Dorothy. I feel I know you: Herb talks a lot about his sisters. I met your handsome son a few minutes ago. I think I have now met everyone except Edward, Steve, Walter and their families."

After dinner, Dorothy said, "I'd better get home and get things ready for tomorrow. You know you two are coming over to my place to meet the rest of the family, don't you?

Herb said, "Seven sharp, we will be there."

CHAPTER 30

A Whole New World

*H*erb and I had entered his home through the front door, but I don't believe we ever used that door again, except when Steve or Donald picked us up in their "auto." It was a two-blocks-shorter walk if you came in through the alley.

Mom had a very small backyard and it was full of beautiful roses. These were the roses Herb had told me about. Mom had never bought a rose bush; they were all started from roses that had been given to her by her children over the years. She would take one of them and plant it in the garden, put a glass jar over it, keep it watered and fertilized, and end up with a rose bush.

This block of row houses was very old. They needed paint on the outside, but maintenance-wise they had been kept up by the tenants. Entering Mom's house from the back door, you walked into a nice-size dining room furnished in antique mahogany furniture which included a curved-glass-front china cupboard filled with beautiful antique china. In the dining room there was one window looking out to the rose garden. The kitchen was an alcove to the left of the door that extended out toward the back of the house.

Between the living room and the dining room was a stairway leading up to the second- and third-floor bedrooms. Mom was a spotless housekeeper. While inside the house, you would not know you were in an old building.

Herb and I slept in his old bedroom on the second floor, looking out over the street to the railroad switching yard. We had a fan in the window, which made it possible to sleep in that hot, humid Baltimore weather. It not only brought in the air, but also cinders from the switching yard.

Early the next morning, we were awakened by the hucksters going up and down the alleys, calling, "Hard crabs alive, fresh fish, hard crabs alive." It was Friday in a predominantly Catholic city, so they didn't take long to sell out and have to go back to re-supply.

Mom and Pop had already eaten when we got down to the dining room, but she had heard us moving around and had our breakfast waiting. We ate in the kitchen and Herb insisted that she sit with us and tell him all about his old friends from the neighborhood: Were they home from the Service yet? Had any of his friends been killed in the war?

After breakfast, Herb took me down the hill to 23rd Street, the Italian neighborhood where he used to play sandlot baseball on the Oak Pleasure Club team. On the way, he started telling me stories of his life in the Italian neighborhood.

"I was the only non-Italian on the team, but they loved me. I was their catcher and we seldom lost a game. The whole neighborhood turned out for every game. One game, I hit a home run, and as I was coming in to home plate, this guy threw a hip into me, sending me rolling."

We had reached 23rd Street, and as we turned the corner, we saw a huge banner stretched over the street between second-story windows, reading, "WELCOME HOME JOE."

It was a hot day and people were sitting on their front steps trying to catch a breath of cool air. Suddenly, someone shouted, "It's Herb! Hey Mom, Herby is home! He has brought his wife to meet us."

People came swarming out of their homes, running toward us. Herb was surrounded by admirers talking in both Italian and English. The mothers of his baseball team were hugging him, laughing and crying; their husbands were trying to shake his hand and welcome him home. Everyone was talking and laughing at once. I realized that Herb hadn't been exaggerating: my husband was famous in Baltimore.

Herb wrapped an arm around me and said, "I told Andy the first stop we were going to make would be to see my old friends on 23rd Street. I guess, since her name isn't Anderson anymore, I should stop calling her Andy. I would like you all to meet my beautiful bride, Ruth 'Anderson' Gunther."

All the attention had shifted to me now. One by one, Herb introduced his friends. Their names were all familiar because Herb had included them on our wedding announcement list. First in line was Mom Lupreato. She could see how overwhelmed I was and, taking my hand, she said, "We have all been waiting for Herb to bring you down to see us so we could welcome you to 23rd Street. My son Joe is running the shop now, but he is going to want to meet you. You two run along and visit, but Herb, you promise you will bring Ruth to my house for lunch with Joe."

Herb promised and we proceeded up the street with the crowd following. We stopped at so many homes as we went: the Vicchio's, Linardy's, Deluca's and the Caetano's, until finally we reached the Denunzio home. By this time, the crowd had grown. Two of the Denunzio girls had already greeted us, but when Herb saw Papa and Mom Denunzio standing at the foot of their stairs, waiting with tears of joy running down their faces, he grabbed my arm and we ran to meet them.

They were a tiny couple and it was their son Joe for whom the banner had been made. After introducing me, Herb said, "Ruth, these two were my most faithful fans when I caught for the Oak Pleasure Club Baseball Team. Remember me telling you about the guy that threw a hip into me as I was coming into home plate? The bleachers emptied onto the field, led by Mom Denunzio. I picked myself up and started back onto the field, but when I saw all those angry Italians out there fighting my battle, I wasn't about to get in the middle of that." Everyone was laughing and adding to the story.

Joe spoke up. "Sis, tell Herb what Ma did to my radio when I went into the Service." Everyone roared with laughter. They had heard the story. One of Joe's sisters volunteered.

"Do you remember how Papa loved to come home, have a couple beers, and listen to Gabe Heater tell about what was happening on the war front? Well, just before enlisting, Joe had bought this beautiful console radio. When he shipped out, Mom took the shears and cut the electric cord right where it entered the radio. She said, 'Nobody's-a-gonna listen to Joe's radio till he comes-a home.'"

"Pa had to hear his news, so he goes out and buys a small radio for himself. Every night he comes home from work, goes to the fridge, gets a beer and goes out on the back porch to listen to Gabe Heater report what our boys are doing in Europe. Gabriel Heater comes on, as he does every night, with 'There is good news tonight,' and proceeds to report the news. 'Everything is looking good for our boys in Europe. Our boys have advanced on the north front and the south; they are pushing the enemy back on all fronts.' Pa calls to his neighbors and says, 'That-a Gabe-a Heater, he's-a-smart-a man he's-a say our boys are winning de war.'"

"This goes on for days and the news is always good until one day Pa comes home, grabs a beer and goes out back. He turns on his radio to hear Gabe's good news, but when Gabe comes on, he says, 'Things aren't going too well for our boys over there. They were pushed back on the north and the south.' Pa jumped up and shouted, 'What the Hell he's-a-know? He sets-a up in that big-a office in New York, he not know nothing 'bout what our boys do.' Pa picked up his radio and slammed it down on the patio, breaking it into pieces."

Even though everyone but Herb and I had heard this story, you wouldn't have known it. Everyone roared with laughter. I would have loved to stay for more of their stories, but we had promised to have lunch with Mom Lupreato. I could understand why Herb loved these people.

The Lupreatos lived next door to their little tavern/store. There was a door connecting the store and home. Herb took me through the store to meet Joe before entering the house. Joe was a short, heavyset, smiling fellow who grabbed Herb in a big bear hug. They had both starred on the Oaks team and were like brothers. Turning to me, Joe said, "Herb, you were right. You told me in your letters you had married a beautiful girl, you lucky guy." He gave me a hug and a kiss on the cheek as he told me what a great guy I had married.

Hanging a "closed" sign on the door, Joe led us into his mother's home. Mom had the table set with assorted slices of meat, bread, cheeses, crackers, fruit, and wine glasses. Mom was waiting. Smiling sweetly, she asked me, "What kind of wine do you like, Ruth, or would you rather have something else?"

I hesitated. I didn't know one wine from the other. Herb spoke up and said, "Give her some of your strong stuff, Mom."

Ignoring him, she smiled at me and said, "I think I know what you would like." Moving to a cabinet, she took out a bottle, opened it and poured a glass for me and one for herself. It was delicious, mild, and slightly sweet. The boys had beer.

After a wonderful lunch and visit, we headed back up the hill. As we passed the switching yard, Herb stopped and pointed to piles of what looked like coal. He said, "When the railroad cars come in at night, they dump the partially burned coal in the yard and load up with new coal for the next day's run. Partially burned coal is coke, and it burns hotter than coal. Some of my buddies and I would take gunny sacks down that hill, fill them with the cooled coke and drag them up the hill. I would sell the coke to the neighbor ladies for twenty five cents a bag. They used the coke in their cook stoves. We weren't supposed to be playing around the switching yard for fear someone would get hurt, so we had to keep an eye out for the railroad guards. I made enough money selling coke to buy my own clothes and help out at home. We sure built up our muscles in a short time. That is probably why I was good in sports. Everyone always thought I was older than I was because I was strong."

We headed on up the hill, and this time we took the alley so Herb could stop by to see Mrs. O'Brian. He said, "Mrs. O'Brian is Mom's best friend. When I was little, if I cut myself, Mom would turn away from the sight of blood and say, 'Go see Mrs. O'Brian.' She would fix me up and send me home. I got so I didn't bother to show Mom. I just went over to see Mrs. O'Brian."

Mom was fixing an early dinner when we got home. I offered to help, but she said, "There isn't anything to do, I am having fish tonight and that takes only a few minutes. Everything else is ready."

After a delicious dinner, Pop did the dishes. He wouldn't let anyone help. "With me in here, there isn't room for anyone else," he laughed.

At dusk, Herb took me for a walk so I could see Baltimore in the evening. We walked the cobbled streets and watched the lamplighter, in his top-hat and tails, light the gas street lamps. Their soft glow lit the walkways of Baltimore. It was like stepping back into history. I was fascinated.

CHAPTER 31

The Gunthers Loved a Party

D orothy lived with her son in a row house with a red brick front, only a short walk from Herb's home. We tried to get Mom to go with us, but she said, "No, you two go along. I'll stay home. I don't like all that beer-drinking."

When we neared Dorothy's place, we could hear the party had started. Herb's brother Walt was standing on the front stoop, waiting for us. He grabbed Herb in a big hug and then greeted me. Herb said, "Ruth, this is my brother Walt. He is two years older than me. When I was little, he and Charles used to throw rocks at me so I wouldn't follow them. He made up for it, though. When I was in college and was able to get a weekend home, I would find money on the nightstand with a note from Walt, saying, 'I know you don't have any money, so I am leaving this for you. I had my good suit cleaned. You can use it.'"

This was Walter, a quiet smiling man that looked much like his brother Charles. You could certainly see that the three of them were their father's sons.

Taking his arm, Walt said, "Herb, you and Ruth have to meet my wife and little girl. Jimmi may bring the baby up for a few minutes, but she won't stay long. The baby goes to bed early."

Walt had met Jimmi while stationed someplace in the South, and married her before going overseas.

We followed Walt into his home. Jimmi was standing in the kitchen with a beautiful little blond girl hugging her leg. Walt proudly introduced his wife and daughter Linda to us. Jimmi greeted us as if she had known us all her life.

"So this is Andy. The family has been talking about nothing else since they heard that Herb was bringing his new bride home to meet us. Herb, I am so happy to finally meet you and Andy. I would know you were Walt's brother if no one had told me, you look so much alike." She proudly introduced little Linda to her aunt and uncle. Linda must have been about sixteen months old. She had been born while Walt was overseas.

Walt picked his daughter up and said, "Come on Jimmi, we can run up to Dorothy's for a little while before you have to put Linda to bed."

Jimmi smiled, but shook her head and, laughing, said, "No, not this late, Walt. I know what your 'little while' turns into." She had a contagious laugh. "I would rather have Ruth and Herb here for dinner some time so we can get acquainted. There will be such a crowd tonight, we won't have a chance to visit. You guys run along and have fun."

We went out the back door, up the alley and into Dorothy's kitchen. Herb's brother Ed and his wife Nellie greeted us at the door with hugs and congratulations. "Sorry the children aren't here, but we will be over at Mom's Sunday after Mass. They are all anxious to see their Uncle Herb and his Navy WAVE."

While we were talking, Steve came through the front door and into the kitchen. He called across the crowd as he tried to get to us, "Herbert, welcome home, you look great." Steve reminded me of a smiling jovial Irishman. He and Ed favored their mother. Although you could tell they were Gunthers, they also had the look of their Irish mother.

Steve had reached us and was hugging his brother. Turning to me, he welcomed me into the family with a hug and a kiss on the cheek. Turning back to Herb, he said, "Herb, the Moose Lodge is having a crab feast tomorrow. I have tickets for you and Andy. You have to come. After the crab feast, we will go to my house so I can introduce Andy to my family."

Herb looked at me. I knew he wanted to go, but I had told him about my trip to San Francisco and seeing those awful-looking crabs. He said, "I don't know Steve. Ruth doesn't eat crab. Do they have anything else to eat?"

Steve said, "I am sure they will have other food, maybe beef sandwiches."

We agreed to go. I did want to meet his family. I had now met all of Herb's siblings. Herb had told me his oldest brother, Frank, had passed away from a heart attack when Herb was in college, leaving a huge hole in the family. Mom never celebrated Christmas after Frank's death. He had always bought them a tree, decorated it and had gifts for all of them. When he died, so did Christmas at Mom's. Frank's wife, Florence, was here, and Herb introduced us. There was no doubt she was one of the family and they dearly loved her.

There was joking, laughter and singing. Pop was right in there with them all. The Gunther men had beautiful voices. Herb had told me about Steve and Ed singing on the radio. Sitting there, watching and listening to the banter back and forth, it was obvious the Gunthers were a very close family.

When they ran low on beer, someone would speak up, "I'll pop for a six pack," and take off up the alley to the corner bar; this was repeated frequently. The more they drank, the louder they got. To my amazement, no neighbors complained: a couple of them did come in and join the party.

Coming from a soft-spoken, non-drinking family, it was a big adjustment for me. The Gunthers all had booming voices and they loved their beer. Since I didn't drink beer, and that was all they offered, they didn't know what to do with me. I kept a glass of coke or iced tea in my hand all evening, hoping no one noticed, but knowing they all did.

We left Dorothy's party around 1:00 AM, completely exhausted. We hadn't caught up on our sleep from the long train ride. My ankles were swollen from too much sitting. I couldn't wait to get to bed. We slept late the next morning.

When we got up, Mom had gone to the market and Pop was waiting for us. He was dressed in white linen trousers, white starched shirt with a very stylish tie to match his suspenders, and wearing a straw Bowler hat. He looked as if he was going to the office, but this was the way he always dressed when he went for his daily walk in Druid Hill Park. Pop was sixty-nine years old, but he carried himself straight and walked like a much younger man.

Mom had left bowls and cereal on the table for us. The coffee was still hot. We had finished eating and had cleaned up the dishes when Mom came in. Herb hurried to take the bags she was carrying. I heard the huckster coming down the alley with his usual call, "Hard Crabs Alive!"

Mom grabbed an old, dented, six-quart aluminum pot with a lid, and her purse, and rushed out. When she came back, she was holding the lid on the pot. I could hear clanking noises in the pot. She had bought a crab and it was trying to get out.

I stood there, watching. She weighted the lid down with a flat iron while she prepared a mixture of vinegar and other seasonings to pour over the crab. Holding the bowl of seasoning in one hand, she removed the flat iron and before she could set it down that crab was out of the pot and headed straight for me, its huge pincher claws raised as if ready to attack. I dashed across the dining room as Mom came after that ugly creature with huge tongs. She chased it clear around the dining room before latching onto it.

Putting it back in the pot with the seasoning, she covered it, weighted the lid and lit the fire under it. Now the clacking really started. I was horrified, "You cook them alive?"

Herb was standing on the stairs, watching and laughing. "You have to cook them alive. If they are dead you don't know if they are spoiled or not. They die quickly in that hot steam."

I had turned to face him and I am sure he could read my mind, "You are taking me to a crab feast???"

Herb said, "Mom, Ruth and I are going over to visit Donald and Mary before Steve gets here. We will be back at eleven thirty. You enjoy your crab."

CHAPTER 32

My First Crab Feast

Herb and I left by the back door and up the alley. I was relieved to get away from that clacking noise and the smell of the crab cooking. It reminded me of Fisherman's Wharf in San Francisco.

Herb wanted me to meet Donald and his parents. It was a short walk to North Avenue, a wide street lined on both sides with huge, three-storied, brownstone row-houses. You could almost smell the wealth.

Mary answered the door and was delighted we had come, but sorry Donald was out. She took us into the parlor where she introduced us to her in-laws.

Mrs. Philbin was a very stylish proper lady and very gracious. Mr. Philbin had some kind of a political job in Washington and traveled back and forth to the Capital daily. He obviously liked Herb and was very proud of his athletic accomplishments. Even though it was a Saturday, he was dressed in a business suit, and although he greeted me warmly, I felt uncomfortable. He seemed to be too aware of my uniform. I thought to myself, "He thinks a woman's place is in the home."

After visiting with Herb, he turned to me and asked about my work as a Corpsman. I explained to him, "We do nursing under the supervision of RN's and doctors. Sometimes we are assigned to work as secretaries for the doctors, or do other office work. I have done all of the above. I am now working in the Property and Accounting Office, keeping track of all the equipment on the base."

He listened politely and then said, "In my traveling around the Capital, I notice that Service men have always gotten preference in seating on public transit. Now women in Service are getting the same preference. Do you think that is right?"

I thought to myself, "You pompous politician," but I asked, "Aren't they doing work in the service of their country? Why should they be treated any different than a man in uniform?"

He puffed up and answered, "Men fight for their country, and they earn that right."

Mary was embarrassed by her rude father-in-law. Standing, she asked, "Herbert, what time is the crab feast Steve was going to take you to? It is after eleven now."

Herb stood up. "Thank you, Mary, I didn't realize it was so late. We had better hurry home. Steve was going to come for us at 11:30." Herb shook Mr. Philbin's hand, but I had hurried over to Mrs. Philbin. She hugged me with an apologetic smile and asked us to come back.

Mary walked us to the door, and we stepped outside. Hugging us both, she whispered an apology.

I smiled and said, "Don't worry about it, Mary. Unfortunately there are many men and women who still cannot accept women in Service. It is too bad they don't bother to talk to us or ask the officers for whom we work. Thanks for stepping up when you did. I was trying to think of a way to get out of there before I said something that might embarrass you and Herb."

She smiled and turned to Herb, "Herbert, if you and Ruth have nothing planned for Wednesday evening, Donald and I would like you to come for dinner."

Herb hugged Mary and asked, "What time should we be here? We have been looking forward to spending some time with you and Donald."

Her smile showed relief, "You can come anytime, but we will eat about six. Come a little early and we can visit. Donald gets home around five-thirty, giving us time for a drink before dinner."

"We will be there," Herb called over his shoulder as he hurried me toward 25th Street. "Ruth, I sure am glad Mary rescued us. I was afraid of what you were about to say."

"You had a right to be. I'll bet he doesn't give his seat to a lady or a Service man. I hope he won't be there Wednesday. I might not be able to hold it if he starts again."

Herb smiled and said, "Don't worry. When Mary and Donald entertain, Mr. and Mrs. Philbin stay in their private quarters on the second floor."

When we reached home, Steve was there visiting with Mom and Pop. He had parked in front of the house. He said, "I hope you had no plans tonight, Mom. I don't know when we will be back. I want to take Ruth and Herb home to meet Katherine and the kids." Mom just smiled and waved us on out the door.

It was a little after twelve when we reached the crab feast. We could hear a band playing behind the fence, along with laughter and loud voices. Steve hurried us through the gate. The party had already started. Men were spreading newspaper over huge, round picnic tables. Steve chose a table for us with some of his friends.

Before Herb reached the table, he was surrounded by a crowd of old fans and admirers from his high school and college days. Most of them he didn't even know, but they knew him. Some were remembering certain boxing matches they had watched him win, both in high school and college. Others remembered certain baseball or football games in which they had seen him excel. They were all trying to get to him to shake their hand and add their memory to the others. Herb was laughing and adding to some of the stories. He was having a great time reminiscing. I was bursting with pride as I listened.

Steve called out, "Hey, Herb, you better get over here before we lose our table." Herb shook a few hands and thanked everyone as he edged his way toward Steve, followed by his admirers who were still reminiscing. When we were seated, I asked, "Were those men all old friends of yours?"

"I don't remember ever meeting any of them. A lot of people in Baltimore knew me from my sports." Putting an arm around me, he laughed and whispered, "Didn't I tell you your husband was famous in Baltimore? You didn't believe me, did you?" Those blue eyes were laughing at me.

As we sat down, I noticed little wooden mallets along with crab crackers at each place. A large man in a white apron proceeded to set mugs of beer before each of us and pitchers of beer on the table. When he came to me, I said, "No thank you, I don't drink beer." He looked at me in disbelief, but skipped to the next person. He left, only to return with a huge pan of steaming crabs. Leaning over the table, he dumped them in the center and started shoving crabs over to each person. When he came to me, I said, "No thank you, I don't eat crabs."

Stepping back, he looked at me and said in a loud voice, "Lady, what in the hell are you doing at a crab feast?"

I joined in the roaring laughter that followed, but thought to myself, "Did Steve fib to me to get us to come, or did he really think they would have sandwiches?"

Of course, there was nothing served other than crabs and beer, and I was starving. Steve said, "I am sorry, Ruth. I was sure they would have sandwiches or something."

Around 4:30, the beer and crabs were gone and everyone was leaving. Steve took us to his home in the suburbs of Baltimore, where I met his children and wife Katherine.

Katherine was a sweet, timid, quiet little lady, not at all what you would have expected an outgoing, life-of-the-party guy like Steve to have chosen, but it was obvious they adored each other. After eating the supper Katherine had prepared for us, I could forgive Steve.

CHAPTER 33

The War Ends

Sunday morning, I attended Mass with Herb. This was the first time we had attended church together. On the base, we each attended our own services. That twinge of guilt crept back into my mind. Herb had served in this church as an altar boy for Father Buckley from his early teens through college. I could not help wondering what was going through his mind. If there was regret, he showed no sign of it in that chiseled face of his.

After Mass, we went back to the house to find Mom preparing a big dinner. The table was set with her finest china. We could smell a roast in the oven. Edward and Nellie were there with their children. They stopped by every Sunday after Mass to see "Momsie and Pops." Ed and Nellie lived on 23rd Street with Nellie's family, the only non-Italian family on the street.

Shortly after Ed and his family left, Charles arrived, followed by Dorothy and her son, Danny. They had come to join us for dinner. It seemed we had gone nonstop since we arrived. Nellie had asked us to come to their home for dinner on Wednesday. We had promised Anna we would be at her place on Monday, Mary's on Tuesday and Walter's on Thursday. It was a good thing Herb didn't have any more sisters and brothers because we were running out of days. We were leaving for Indiana on Friday the 17th, a two-day train ride. Our leave was flying by.

During the day, Herb took me sightseeing around Baltimore. Monday, we walked through Druid Hill Park, a beautiful 740-acre park purchased by the City of Baltimore with a one-cent streetcar tax. We visited Wyman Park and the Baltimore Museum of Art, where he pointed out the lions that stood on large bases on either side of the entry, as if to guard the place. A sign named the artist who designed them, but it didn't name Herb's father, Stephen Gunther, the stonemason who carved them.

Tuesday, August 14th, we went to Lexington Market. I had never been in an open-air market before and could not believe the size of this one. It was huge. Herb said, "This is where Mom used to come once or twice a week to shop. I always knew which days she shopped here. When I got out of school, I would run to the streetcar stop and wait for her so she wouldn't have to carry her groceries home.

"The summer before entering college, one of my high school friends and I worked in the fresh-meat department in this market. One day our boss came over and said, 'We have an oversupply of chickens hanging on hooks over there. I want you boys to try to push the chickens. If they don't sell today, they won't be good tomorrow and I will have to toss them.'

"My friend Joe was a born salesman and could have made it as a standup comedian. He was always joking with the customers and knew many of them by name. When the boss left, I looked around for possible buyers and said, 'Joe, how are we going to sell all these chickens?'

"'No problem, Herby. Watch the expert. I'll show you how to sell these chickens,' he said, as he looked around for a prospect. He honed in on the first lady that came by and said, 'Good morning, Mum. You look lovely this morning. May I help you? I'll bet you are looking for something for dinner tonight.'

"Joe was a handsome guy and could charm the ladies. She smiled at him and said, 'Thank you, young man. Yes, I am looking for something for dinner. Do you have a suggestion?'

"'I have just the thing,' he said, as he lifted two of the chickens from their hooks and held them out in front of the lady, saying, 'How about these nice fresh chickens?'

"Her smile faded as she looked at the chickens, 'Those chickens don't look fresh to me. How long have they been hanging there? They sure are scrawny things.'

"Joe was undaunted. Pulling back the chickens as if to protect them he said softly, 'Madam, Please don't speak that way of the dead.'"

We were both laughing, "Did you sell the chickens?" I asked.

Herb laughed, "I don't remember."

We left the market and Herb was pointing out things he thought would interest me when we heard shouting. Buildings emptied out onto the street. Everyone was shouting, "THE WAR IS OVER, THE WAR IS OVER, JAPAN HAS SURRENDERED, THE WAR IS OVER!" Cars were racing by with people on top and on running boards or hanging out of the windows.

It was a strange feeling to be standing there on a street corner in Baltimore, in uniform, away from the base and our friends, when we got this wonderful news. When we left the hospital, we knew it was only a matter of time before Japan would surrender, but for some reason it didn't seem real. I looked at Herb and asked, "Do you feel as if the war is over?"

"No, not really," he said. "Maybe it is because we aren't on base or with others in uniform and hearing them shouting. The people we are watching are civilians and I keep thinking maybe someone started a rumor and they may not actually know." We watched the celebrating for a while and then worked our way through the crowds, headed for Mary's home.

I was delighted to find that Donald was nothing like his father. He was a kind, gentle man who greeted us at the door, hugging us both and asking, "Have you heard the war is over? Offices closed early and everyone is celebrating. I was in Washington D.C. when the news came. The city went wild."

Mary seated us in the parlor, served drinks, and we visited. Donald and Mary had helped raise Herb. He was more like a son than a brother or brother-in-law. Donald asked, "Herbert, do you have plans or do you know what you want to do when you get out of the Service?"

"I plan on getting a teaching and coaching job someplace," he answered. "I have checked Baltimore schools and they only pay $1600.00 a year. If we stay in California, I will make $1800, but I will have to get a California Teaching Credential. We like California, so it looks like we will be staying there. The GI Bill will pay for the year of graduate school I will need."

After a wonderful dinner and evening, we thanked Mary, said our goodbyes and headed home.

CHAPTER 34

Herb Meets the Anderson Clan

*F*riday morning, we boarded the train to Chicago. Arriving there around one the next day, we transferred to the Monon Train. When we reached Monticello, Wayne and Mom were standing on the platform as our train rolled in.

What a wonderful sight! Wayne was still in uniform. His face was healed, but the scar on his jaw was very evident. He lifted me off the train step and gave me a crushing hug. He was solid muscle. I tried unsuccessfully to hold back the tears. Looking at me, he laughed that musical laugh of his and said, as he extended his hand to Herb, "Is this my new brother-in-law you have been bragging about?" With his jaw still wired shut, it was difficult to understand him when he spoke.

Mom stood smiling as she waited for us. After giving me a hug, she turned to Herb and said, "Herb, I want to welcome you into our family. I hope you and Ruth will be as happy as her father and I were."

Herb smiled, leaned over and hugged her, saying, "Thank you, Mom. I love your daughter very much and I promise I will be a good husband to her."

Wayne and Herb retrieved our luggage and loaded it into Mom's old Studebaker. Mom climbed into the front seat, chatting about everyone in the family. She said, "The twins are working, Lois and Jo are at home waiting, Martha is off someplace with her boyfriend and Bob is collecting for his paper route. They will all be here for supper. Everyone wants to meet the new addition to the Clan."

When we reached the house, Grandpa Arrick was waiting on the porch.

Grandpa Carmi Arrick

I stepped out of the car and hurried to greet him. Grandpa was a short, square-built man with a prominent Roman nose and a ready smile. His thick, curly, once-red hair was now a rusty grey. He had been a farmer, a contractor, County Assessor and could quote more Bible than any minister I ever met. He dearly loved his children and grandchildren, and they loved him. Now in his eighties, he still baked Grandma's Sugar Cookies for his grandchildren and his neighbor's children.

I proudly introduced Herb to Grandpa, who studied him as he smiled and extended his hand. "Ruth wrote me all about you. If you can live up to her description, you are okay with me."

"I plan to try," Herb said, as he shook the work-worn hand.

When we went inside, Jo, 10, and Lois, 12, rushed to hug me, but they were a little bashful when I introduced them to their new brother-in-law. It didn't take long, though, before they were standing close to him, showing him their projects and taking him outside to meet their dog, Red.

Martha, now 16 and never bashful, was dropped off by her boyfriend. She rushed in shouting, "Hey, Ruth, where is that handsome guy you have been bragging about?" She barely hugged me, stepped past me and was shaking Herb's hand. "I'm Martha," she said. "I had almost given up on Ruth finding any-one good enough for her. I am glad she finally did." Herb was a little taken aback, but laughed and greeted her.

While Mom and the girls prepared dinner, I had a chance to talk to Wayne. I said, "I have waited months for you to fill in the cut-out holes in those letters you wrote me from overseas. One letter said, 'It wasn't my head that got it that second day on _____.'"

Wayne chuckled, "It was our second day on Manila. I had my mortar set up on a hill when the Sergeant ordered everyone down the hill. Something told me to wait. The rest of the guys had started down when machinegun fire came from three nests on the next hill. Those who had started down the hill were being mowed down. I took out the first machine gun nest, moved quickly with my mortar and shell carrier to another location, and took out the second one. I jumped to a new location and a mortar shell exploded nearby. I felt something hot hit my backside. It burned like crazy. I was too busy to check my burning seat. I had to take out that third machine gunner. I didn't have time to set up the mortar, so I used my knee as a base, taking out the third nest. When I had time to check, I found the seat of my pants was gone." Wayne's voice broke slightly as he said softly, "and so was my shell carrier. The next day, we found his ruby ring and parts of his pack on the hillside."

You could have heard a pin drop when he finished. I broke the silence: "I am surprised you didn't blow your knee out."

Laughing, he said, "I didn't have time to think about that. I just knew I had to take out that other nest."

I quickly changed the subject. "Have they given you a time-frame for when you might get your teeth?" I asked.

"They aren't in any hurry. They want to be sure the bone graft has taken. I am still spitting up pieces of shrapnel that have worked their way out of my jaw, tongue and throat. This has caused swelling and slowed the healing process," he answered.

Martha spoke up, "What medals did you earn besides the Purple Heart, Wayne?"

Wayne smiled and said, "I know it is hard to believe, but I earned the Good Conduct Medal. I also earned several marksmanship awards."

It was years later that I learned Wayne had been awarded three Bronze Stars for bravery while serving in the Philippines, but he never mentioned these honors to anyone.

I excused myself and went out to help Mom. She handed me a letter to read. It was from Wayne's Sergeant. The following is an excerpt from that letter.

Philippines
June 7, 1945

Dear Mother Anderson,

Perhaps you may not remember me, but I was your son's Platoon Sgt. for a long time. I had the pleasure of visiting with you, your son Art, and his wife at Camp Polk, remember?

Mom, the purpose of writing this letter is to tell you what a grand son you have and about the splendid job he did over here. It was indeed a privilege to serve with him and to see the courage he displayed on many occasions. He was always the first to go in and the last to come out. Together we gave those Jap machine guns hell. He did the shooting and I did the observing. Don't know who will help me now: seems as though my right arm is gone. One morning Wayne knocked out two machine guns in about four minutes of action. Later on, he made several trips into heavy artillery fire to bring out equipment that we badly needed. For that I have recommended him for the Silver Star. He is truly a soldier among soldiers.

With loving memories,
Always your friend,
Everett W. Albright

Bobby, now fourteen, came dragging in from his paper route. He smiled broadly as he hugged me and wished me happiness.

Hearing us, Herb came out from the living room and said, "You must be Bob. I am Herb. Ruth has told me about you and how hard you work. I am glad to finally meet you. I never had a paper route, but from the time I was 7 or 8, I worked at any job I could get to make money and help out at home."

Bob smiled broadly and followed Herb into the living room. I heard Herb say, "Ruth tells me you play basketball. I never got to play that game because it overlapped with my boxing and football seasons." They chatted on about sports and school. Herb had made a hit with my family.

Just as we got dinner on the table and were being seated, the twins, Mary and Margaret, came in from work to join us. Hugs and introductions started all over again.

There was a food grinder fastened to the table, next to Wayne's plate. Looking at Herb, he grinned and said, "I have to have my food pre-chewed until my jaw heals and I get my new teeth. I don't mind, though. It is still Mom's cooking and I made it home."

Mom spoke up, "I offered to grind it in the kitchen but he wouldn't let me. He said my cooking was more than enough."

After Grandpa said grace and food was being passed, I watched Wayne choose a large piece of chicken, bone it and feed it through the grinder, followed by steamed vegetables. Even his salad went through the grinder. He spooned mashed potatoes onto his plate beside the meat and covered them with gravy. Looking up, he saw me watching. He grinned and said, "It tastes the same and I don't have to chew my food." Everyone laughed with him.

Sunday morning, we all went to the Presbyterian Church. Mom said proudly, "Herb, this church is over 150 years old. My grandparents helped to organize it. In the beginning they met in a pasture west of Monticello until they could get land and build here."

I was afraid she was going to ask him what church he belonged to. Fortunately some of my friends rushed over to greet me and to meet Herb. I knew the time would come, but I prayed Mom would have a chance to know Herb first.

After church, we hurried home to find my brother Raymond and his wife Ellen, my best friend, waiting for us with their two boys. Herb had now met all my siblings except Arthur, Esther and Mabel. Mabel was out of the Marines and was living in Texas with her husband, Howard. Arthur and Esther would no doubt be over after dinner. The table was at its full size, now seating sixteen.

Mom had put a huge roast in the oven before leaving for church. Peeled potatoes were ready to put on to boil and mash. She opened a couple of quarts of her home-canned green beans and set them on the stove. Mom had made Jell-O salad with ground-up fruit the night before. I made the gravy and Wayne carved the roast. In no time, dinner was on the table. No one touched anything until Grandpa said grace.

After dinner, the leftovers were put away and dishes carried to the kitchen to be washed later. It was a tradition with our family that every Sunday afternoon we gathered around the piano and sang as Mom played. We had been blessed with good voices and we all sang. Mom and Grandpa both had beautiful voices. Grandpa had sung in the church choir as far back as I could remember; I think we got that gene from him. Herb fit right in with his deep baritone.

While we were singing, Arthur and his wife Imogene arrived. Herb and I stepped out onto the porch to greet them and be able to visit.

Arthur had graduated from veterinary medical school as a Lieutenant in the Army Reserves. He reported for active duty and, to his surprise, he didn't pass the physical because of high blood pressure. He came home and took up where my father had left off as a veterinarian. The farmers who had known my father were waiting for him. Arthur had big shoes to fill.

While we were talking, my sister Esther arrived. She introduced us to her new husband, Ed Brothers, and I introduced Herb.

Arthur took my arm and, moving me toward the door, he said, "Let's all go in and join the choir. It's been a long time since so many of us have sung together. We are all here except Mabel and Howard."

Mom beamed as we rejoined the family. She had eleven of her twelve children, two daughters-in-law, two sons-in-law and Grandpa surrounding her as she played.

I wondered what Herb thought of my family: it was so different from his. His was an older family. He had nieces and nephews older than my younger siblings. We were a soft-spoken, fun-loving family that teased each other, loved a good joke and laughed a lot; however, alcohol, gambling, cards, or tobacco were never seen in Mom's house. Raymond smoked and drank, but never in front of Mom.

I warned Herb not to light up his pipe in the house. If he smoked it, he stepped out onto the porch. Grandpa liked Herb, but he eyed that pipe with disapproval. He believed that smoking or drinking was breaking God's commandment, "The body is the temple of the soul and thou shalt keep it holy."

When our voices began to give out, one by one my family excused themselves, wished us happiness, thanked Mom for the wonderful dinner and left. Mom and the girls went to the kitchen to clean up the dishes while Herb and I visited with Wayne.

I took a notepad from my purse and showed him a calendar where I had written the time and date when I had dreamt he had been injured. I told him about the dream in detail. I said, "I prayed for you most of what was left of that night until I fell asleep from exhaustion."

He couldn't believe it. He said, "We had a bunch of Filipino workers in camp, when suddenly they all disappeared. We didn't trust them. They would work for whoever paid them the most. There were about twenty of us and we started digging in for the night when a mortar shell dropped in the middle of us. Only three of us survived: a dark-haired man, another redhead and me."

As close as Wayne could figure, I was dreaming at the time he had been hit. He said, "That gives me a creepy feeling. Your dream was so much like what happened. And for two guys from here to just appear and save my life, God must not be ready for me. Remember those Testaments that Aunt Winona gave us when we entered the Service? Well, I never read the Bible much before I went in, but I nearly wore that Bible out on the battlefield." As he spoke, he pulled the worn Bible from his breast pocket. "I kept it in this pocket over my heart." Grinning, he added, "I kept a silver dollar in it, just in case God needed a little help." I doubt that he had, but the story got him a good laugh.

Herb excused himself and went to the kitchen to visit with Mom and the girls while Wayne and I continued talking. This gave us a chance to exchange war stories. Wayne asked, "Are there things that bring back memories of your patients?"

"Oh yes," I answered. "I can walk down the street and look into people's eyes and tell you if a person is haunted by horrible memories. One memory I can't shake is that of putrefying burned flesh. Just thinking about it, I can smell it."

Wayne nodded in understanding and said, "For me, it is the smell of blood on the battlefield."

I saw Herb cross the dining room and head upstairs. Looking at my watch, I said, "It's after ten. I guess Herb decided to go on up to bed. I am tired, too. I'll see you in the morning, Wayne."

When I got up to our room, Herb was lying across the bed, looking very sad. Sitting down beside him, I asked, "Is something wrong?"

Pulling himself up to sit beside me, he said. "Your mother was telling me all about the seven generations of Presbyterian ministers in her family prior to her generation, and she asked, 'and what church do you belong to, Herb?' When I said 'Catholic,' she turned white as a sheet, didn't say anything for a while, and then asked, 'Were you married Catholic?' When I said no, she seemed to relax, but I felt terrible."

"I am sorry I wasn't there to tell her why we hadn't told her," I said.

The next morning, I was up and dressed before Herb and hurried downstairs, hoping to get a chance to talk to Mom before the family was up. Walking into the kitchen, I found her making coffee. She looked tired and I guessed she hadn't slept well. Looking up, she asked, "Why didn't you tell me Herb was Catholic?"

"Mom, I wanted you to know Herb before we told you he was Catholic. Because I wouldn't sign papers to raise my children Catholic, we could not be married by a Priest. Herb had been an altar boy from childhood through college, and it was difficult for him. He loved his church, but he decided he loved me too much to let the church split us up. We were married by a Presbyterian Minister in a non-denominational church. As long as I live, I can never make that up to him."

Mom was studying me. "He must love you very much," she said, as she turned and continued preparing breakfast.

When Herb stepped into the kitchen, Mom smiled as she walked over to him and said, "Herb, I want you to know that your religion makes no difference in my feelings toward you. I think my daughter made a great choice and I am happy with that choice."

Herb hugged her and said, "Thank you, Mom."

CHAPTER 35

Our Unusual Wedding Shower

*B*etty and Leigh Stair came to see me and to meet Herb. I introduced them and said to Herb, "I was at Betty and Leigh's home when I first heard the news of the attack on Pearl Harbor. Betty and I have been close friends since grade school."

Betty and Leigh Stair

Betty smiled and said, "Leigh and I want to have a wedding shower for you two. There aren't many of our classmates still here in Monticello, but we have invited those that are. We planned for Sunday afternoon, so those who are working will be able to come. Leigh will pick you up around two if that is okay. It will give us a little time to visit before the rest come. I thought it would be fun to have a picnic in the pasture if the weather is good."

"Betty, that sounds wonderful," I said. "I doubt that my City Boy has ever been on a real farm. Are you game, Herb?"

Herb grinned and said, "Sounds like fun to me." Then his expression changed and he asked hesitantly, "There won't be cows in that pasture, will there?"

They laughed, and Leigh said, "Not close enough to bother you, Herb."

It was a beautiful Sunday morning. The weather was perfect, not too hot. We attended church with the family and after lunch we joined in the singing until Leigh arrived to take us to the farm.

Betty had prepared baskets of fried chicken, salads and gallons of fresh lemonade. While we visited, Leigh and Herb took turns at the crank on the ice-cream freezer. When it was frozen, Betty removed the dasher. Leigh packed it with more ice and covered it with an old blanket to allow it to set up and stay frozen.

Betty said, "Leigh, I think we had better load all this stuff in the pickup and start for the pasture. The girls will be arriving soon." Leigh and Herb loaded the food along with bottles of water and a stack of blankets into the back of his pickup. The four of us climbed into the front seat and headed across the fields. We could see cattle grazing way on the far side of the pasture.

Leigh set up a card table on which he placed paper plates, cups, napkins and plastic flatware. Soon cars began to arrive. I greeted my old friends and introduced them to Herb.

After we visited for a while, Leigh opened the back of the pickup and Betty handed out blankets.

Herb watched as the girls began to spread blankets on the grass. He had never been on a farm and I doubt that he had ever been on a picnic. In fact, I had never before been to a wedding shower in a pasture. I was thrilled that mine was the first.

As I spread my blanket, I noticed a thistle in the grass and managed to spread the blanked so the thistle would be under where Herb would sit. Betty looked at me, frowning, and said, "That is a thistle you just spread your blanket over."

I smiled and said, "I know."

Leigh uncovered the food on the back of the pickup and said, "Come on, Herb. You and Ruth lead your guests through the food line."

Betty was a wonderful cook, and everything she prepared had been raised on their farm.

Carrying our food to our blanket, I sat down, carefully avoiding the thistle as Herb came to join me. Betty was watching with a concerned look on her face. Herb sat down and immediately jumped up. Everyone was laughing.

Pulling the blanket back, revealing the thistle, he looked at me, grinning, and said, "You did that on purpose, didn't you?" I laughed and nodded as I re-laid the blanket, this time avoiding the thistle.

We began unwrapping gifts. None were lavish or expensive. These were hard times, and very little was available to purchase if you had the money. Betty's mother had bought a towel and washcloth around the edges of which she had crocheted to make them special.

We laughed, joked and told stories about each other. I was delighted that Herb was joining in and having a good time. I could not have had a better wedding shower.

It was dusk when we finished eating, and my friends began to leave. Herb and I helped Betty and Leigh pack up everything and take it back to the house.

As we drove, I said, "I can't thank you two enough. This was the most wonderful shower I have ever attended, and the most original. I loved every minute of it."

Herb spoke up, "I have had a lot of new experiences since I met Ruth. I was married in a cemetery and attended our wedding shower in a pasture." Everyone laughed. "My friends in Baltimore wouldn't believe it, but I wouldn't change any of it. I loved it all and really want to add my thanks to Ruth's. You guys are the best."

Betty beamed and Leigh said, "We enjoyed it as much as you, Herb. We are so glad Ruth found a guy like you."

After putting the food away and visiting for awhile, Betty and Leigh drove us back to Monticello. Herb and Leigh were in the front seat, talking sports. I was pleased they were becoming good friends. Betty and I were still reminiscing when we reached Mom's house. We hugged them both and thanked them again before going inside.

Wayne, Mom, Herb and I had visited all our friends and relatives. Herb and I spent as much time with Wayne as we could. He never talked about combat unless he was asked a question.

When we were alone, I asked, "Wayne, does it bother you talking about the war? I know my patients wanted to talk about their combat experiences, and we were happy to listen. I think some of them may have embellished the stories a little as they repeated them over and over, but there was no doubt they had been through hell. Their stories of hand-to-hand combat sent chills down my spine."

He smiled and said, "It isn't that soldiers don't want to talk about the war, but since no one asks us, we figure they aren't interested in hearing about it. When we are with other military personnel, we talk about our experiences with each other.

"The closest I came to hand-to-hand combat was in Manila. As you know, Japanese fighters hide in tunnels underground. We had taken an area on Manila and were looking for stragglers. Seeing some sheets of corrugated metal lying on the ground, I carefully raised the edge of one of the sheets with my bayonet. When I saw the ends of guns being raised, I emptied my rifle into that hole before flipping it off. That was close enough for me."

Our thirty-day Leave was coming to an end. The family all gathered at the station to send us off. It was hard saying goodbye to them. Who knew what our future held or when we would see them again. We were anxious to get back and find out when we would be discharged; but then what? Our paychecks would end and we had decided to stay in California. I was having morning sickness and knew I was pregnant. We wanted a family, but had hoped to wait until we were settled. We had no savings, and with so many military leaving the Service at one time, we knew jobs were going to be hard to find. If Herb was worried, he didn't show it.

I remembered hearing my father advising a young man about marrying his long-time girlfriend before finding a job. "Well," he said, "You might be able to live on love for a little while, but after that you get hungry just like every one else." We had just spent what little we had been able to save on our thirty-day leave.

CHAPTER 36

Mixed Emotions

O ur trip back to the base was exciting though uneventful. The train was full of discharged Service people heading home after long separations from their friends and family. Excitement ran high.

We arrived in California on September 3rd and went to our apartment. It was wonderful to be home again.

The next morning, we caught the bus to the base and reported in. The Personnel Officer told us we would be discharged based on how long we had been in the Service, but if we wanted to stay in, we would get a step-up in rate the day we signed over. I was to be discharged September 21st, but Herb would have to wait until December 23rd.

Stopping at the Post Office to pick up our saved mail, we found a new Postmaster on duty. I asked about Roy and was told he had been discharged and had returned to his job as Postmaster in Fresno, California. In our stack of mail was a note from Kenny. He had been discharged and was on his way home to Montana.

Having decided to eat our meals on base until my discharge in order to save money, we headed to the Chow Hall for breakfast before reporting to duty.

When I arrived at my office, I was shocked to see that most of my friends had been discharged and new, younger faces had taken their place. I felt as if I had lost my family. My friends would be scattered across the country from coast to coast, taking up their lives where they had left off. Would I ever see them again? I was happy to see that the civilian workers were still there, and they greeted me warmly.

Back at my quarters, things hadn't changed. Most of the WAVES were still there. Most of us had arrived together, and we would be discharged together.

On September 21st, as we drove through the gate for the last time, the girls were quiet. We were filled with mixed emotions, rejoicing that the war was over and we were going home, but sad that we would be scattering like birds. I had loved my time in the Service and would miss it and all my friends.

It seemed so long ago that these young women had joined the WAVES. We were different people now. We spoke a different language and felt a complete disconnect from civilians. Through our patients, we had lived the war. We had seen blood, suffering and death. We had heard stories we would never repeat, but would never forget.

Being accustomed to dressing like all the other WAVES and being told which uniform to wear and when to wear it, I had paid no attention to style changes. During our time in the Service, our skirts had gone up from calf length to knee-high. We had been told this was to save scarce material during the war. Other than that, there had been no change in our uniforms.

When I was in uniform, I blended into the crowd of WAVES. Now, when I wore my civilian dresses, I felt that I stood out and everyone was looking at me. The few dresses that I had brought back with me were outdated, and with a baby on the way, we didn't have money to buy new clothes.

When discharged, I was paid for a trip back to my home in Indiana, and Herb would be paid for a return trip to Maryland. We agreed to set this money aside for our moving expenses and the anticipated doctor and hospital costs.

Herb had only three more months before his discharge, and we had no idea where we would be moving or if he would be able to find work.

The three months pay Herb would have coming before his discharge would have to pay our expenses until he found work. I could not help worrying, but I planned my meals carefully, bought nothing extra and stretched every dollar. We never went out to dinner or a movie. I removed the stripes from my uniform shirts and jackets and wore them as long as I could.

Except for one year in college, I hadn't been without a job and a paycheck since I was sixteen. I had become used to working nine to sixteen hours a day and feeling productive.

Setting up my sewing machine, I made baby clothes and blankets. I learned to crochet and edged the blankets with a little shell design to make them special. In spite of this, the days dragged and I was bored.

I missed our meeting at the Chow Hall for lunch, but Herb was happy to come home to find me with dinner on the table. I only once took the bus to the base to meet him, thinking I would be allowed through the gate to see the few friends I had left there, but I was told that only those on active duty and civilian workers were allowed on the base. I had to wait outside the gate for Herb. As I waited, I watched, hoping to see someone I knew among those rushing through the gate on liberty. I didn't see one familiar face. I was overcome by a strange lonely feeling which vanished when I saw Herb's smiling face approaching. We caught a ride back to the apartment, but after that I chose to wait at the apartment for Herb.

On Oct. 31st, we put out a bowl of candy just in case some little goblins ventured up our stairs for Trick or Treat. I was just ready to serve dinner when there was a knock on the door. Herb opened it to three young boys. "Trick Or Treat!" they shouted in unison.

Herb, holding the bowl of candy, smiled at them and asked, "What will you do if you don't get a treat?"

"Soap your windows," one responded.

Feeling safe in a second floor apartment, Herb laughed and said, "Go ahead."

Without hesitation the young man stepped in front of Herb, crossed the living room and soaped my nice clean window. Herb roared with laughter and gave them their treat.

When they left, I said to Herb, "Your treat will be cleaning that window."

He was still laughing as he put an arm around me and said, "I don't mind. It was worth it. I was thinking. 'He can't soap a second-story window.' I just wanted to see what he would do. He is a smart kid."

Herb made good use of his time while waiting for his discharge. In early October, he got a one-day pass and went to the Claremont Men's College to sign up for classes necessary for his California teaching credential. He filled out papers for admission in January and asked if they knew of any work he could apply for.

They referred him to a Government Housing Project in nearby Upland.

When he got home, he had been admitted to the college and had signed a rental agreement for a two-bedroom, unfurnished apartment in the Los Olivos Housing Project. This project consisted of several groupings of three duplexes. Each grouping formed a U-shape around a nice-sized courtyard facing out to the street. The project had been built by the government to house defense workers, and was full of children. Their Recreation Director had resigned and Herb would be taking over that job beginning Jan 2, 1946. The pay would just cover our rent and maybe a little more. His GI Bill money should start in January and we would be able to buy some furniture and eat. Our prayers were being answered.

CHAPTER 37

Civilians Again

*I*n mid December, I answered a knock at my door. When I opened it, there stood Vi in her uniform. "Lady, do you think you might have a spare bed for a tired old Veteran?" she asked in that slow Texas drawl of hers.

I let out a shriek of joy and we were hugging, laughing, talking, and crying at the same time. I said, "Oh Vi, you can't know how welcome this visit is. I have been so lonely for my old Navy friends. Herb is going to be so happy to see you. He gets out the 23rd and is prancing at the bit. He can hardly wait. If Kenny were here it, would be perfect.

Vi, laughing at my running on, said, "I spent a couple days with Ernie and Marie after we landed in L.A. They told me about your plans and send their love. Marie said when you get settled in Upland, they are going to drive down to see you. After leaving there, I caught that old milk train here."

I said, "Yes, Marie and I have been writing to each other. Rose and Vern also have promised to visit. We spent the afternoon exchanging news about our Navy friends, where they were and what they were doing.

We walked to the market, where I introduced Vi to Chuck. I remembered Vi's favorite meal was broiled pork chops and mashed turnips, so I bought pork chops and turnips for dinner.

Dinner was ready when Herb came in and gave me a kiss. Vi stepped out of the kitchen and said, "Hi, you old goat."

"Mop head, where did you come from?" he asked, as he grabbed and hugged her. "You are a sight for sore eyes. Ruth and I figured you would be getting your discharge soon. I assume you are headed home to El Paso, but I am so glad you stopped here first. I am sure you have brought Ruth up on the news of our friends, but you will have to repeat it over dinner. Ruth is the letter writer in our family."

We visited until late that night. The next morning, after an early breakfast, I said a tearful goodbye to Vi as she left with Herb carrying her bag.

When they reached the train, Vi choked up as she gave Herb a hug and wished him everything good in the future. She boarded the milk train to Riverside where she would transfer to a train to El Paso. Shouting his goodbye, Herb ran to catch the bus to the base.

The day after Vi left, Herb was walking on air when he left home. Once he reached the base, he would board a bus to a discharge center in the Los Angeles area, where he would learn what was available to veterans after their discharge.

Unlike me, Herb never liked the Service. He served because he loved his country and it was his duty to serve. Now that the war was over, he was anxious to get on with his life. Unlike many veterans, he had no job to go back to. Like many other young men, he had lost the greatest opportunity of his life because of the war. While in college, he had been drafted to play Major League Baseball after he graduated. When Pearl Harbor was attacked and he was classified 1-A in the Draft, that offer was withdrawn. At age twenty-six, he was considered too old for a career in baseball. He accepted this fact and now just wanted the opportunity to find a school where he could coach and be able to take care of his family.

It was Sunday, December 23, 1946. Herb would be home this evening, a happy civilian. Wanting to surprise him with a Discharge celebration, I went to visit our butcher. Chuck had become a good friend, and even now, with me in civilian clothes and no stamps, he took care of us. As I entered the store, I saw him standing behind the meat counter, just finishing with another customer. He was a nice-looking, sturdily built man in his mid- to late forties. His dark hair was beginning to turn grey.

"Hi Andy," he called to me. "Isn't today the day Herb gets out? I'll bet you are looking for something good to fix for a special dinner to celebrate. I have a nice roast that needs to be used today; I was just getting ready to mark it down." As he spoke, he lifted a beautiful roast from the case and, taking a marker from his pocket, he proceeded to mark the price down almost in half.

I knew that roast was a gift to us, but he didn't want to embarrass me. I took the roast, paid him, and said, "Chuck, you have been wonderful to us. Without you, Herb and I would have had a rough time. I don't know how we can ever thank you."

"Think nothing of it. That is the least I can do. I loved helping you out. Herb told me you will be moving to Upland January 1st. I sure am going to miss you kids.

"Yes, we are moving and we certainly will miss you, but we will see you before we move."

He put an arm over my shoulders, smiled at me and said, "See that you do, young lady. Have Herb stop by. I will save some apple boxes and orange crates for you to pack things in. My wife and I used boxes for end tables and makeshift shelves when we were first married. We also moved into an unfurnished apartment when we were married."

"What a great idea. The Nelsons are lending us their pickup to move what little we have. I was going to ask you for cardboard boxes, but those will work so much better. We owe you so much already, Chuck." I leaned over, kissed him on his furrowed cheek, and hurried out before he saw the tears in my eyes.

When I got home from shopping, I had a quick lunch and then made an apple pie. When it was done, I put the roast in the oven. While it cooked, I set my card table up under the window in the living room, covered it with a "surveyed" Navy linen tablecloth, and set it with our USN-monogrammed silver, our beautiful Corona Hardware plates, glasses and paper napkins.

To make it look more festive, I placed a Christmas candle in the center of the table. We couldn't spare the money for a tree, so this would have to do. Everything looked beautiful.

Satisfied that everything was taken care of, I lay down for a nap while the roast cooked.

It was dusk when I heard the outside door open and Herb taking the steps two at a time. He burst in wearing a huge smile, dropped his bag and grabbed me around the waist, swinging me in a wide circle. "How long has it been since you were kissed by a civilian, Mrs. Gunther?" he asked as he kissed me over and over.

"That was a long three days away from my sweet wife, but I am home and I am free. I am a civilian." I was being swung in a circle again. I knew Herb would not have a hard time adjusting to civilian life.

As he set me down, he saw the table and kissed me again, saying, "That is beautiful and I am starved."

I didn't want to let him go. I said, "The past three days have been the longest three days of my life. I have been taking my walks alone and I hate it. How about if I put the potatoes on low to cook and we take a walk before it gets too dark? They should be almost ready to mash when we get home."

Smiling down at me, he said, "Our first walk as civilians. I have been looking forward to that. I'll stow my gear while you put the potatoes on."

We took a long walk and returned by a different route, talking and laughing as we walked hand in hand. Without warning, two huge dogs came through a hedge, barking, growling and baring their teeth. Herb grabbed me and held me in front of him as we stood frozen. I heard a stern voice calling the dogs, and they disappeared back into the hedge.

I felt Herb's grip on my arm loosen and I turned to look at him. He smiled sheepishly and said, "Ruth, you know no self-respecting dog would bite an expectant mother."

We both laughed, and then he confessed that he had been terrified of dogs all his life. He said, "When I was in elementary school, there was a huge dog that waited for me every day. It hid behind a fence, and when I went through our gate into the alley, it chased me all the way to school. I have never gotten over that fear. I just freeze when a dog comes near me." He smiled and added, "Maybe that helped me later in sports. I am a fast runner."

"Well, you did tell me you were a certified coward," I teased.

"Only when it comes to dogs and mortar shells," he protested. "I will have to show you my scrapbooks. I was written up in the Baltimore Sun for saving a girl from being raped by a big man on the streets of Baltimore. The headlines read, 'Herb Gunther, well known Poly Athlete, saves young woman from attacker.'" I was still teasing him when we reached home.

Herb put the salads and drinks on the table and lit the candle while I took out the roast, mashed the potatoes and made the gravy. Because of the size of the table, we served our plates in the kitchen. When we were seated, we held hands as we thanked God for our many blessings. The war was over, we were healthy, our baby was due in mid-March, we had an apartment to go to, a job waiting for Herb, and GI Bill money would be coming to pay for his school and our living expenses. Our new life was just beginning.

Christmas Eve, Herb and I walked all over town, admiring the wonderful Christmas decorations, ending up at the Catholic Church where we attended Mass. We had been going to the Catholic Church one Sunday, and since there was no Presbyterian Church in Corona, we went to the Methodist Church the next Sunday.

Christmas day, I fixed a huge breakfast and we exchanged one gift each, even though we had agreed, "no gifts this year." Herb bought me a maternity dress and I bought him a shirt.

I had purchased a large roasting hen from a local farmer and we had a wonderful early-afternoon Christmas dinner with all the trimmings. We spent the day eating, walking and playing Rummy. Who could ask for anything more?

The following day, Mrs. Nelson loaned us her truck and gave us a stack of old newspapers to use for wrapping our dishes. She cautioned, "Herb, be careful. The brakes need work and I haven't had the money to take care of them. You just have to pump them a few times to stop." Herb thanked her and we went on to pick up boxes from Chuck.

December 31st, we walked over to Chuck's store to tell him goodbye and to stock up on a few things we would need in our new home. I bought enough meat, eggs and milk to fill our ice chest. Herb had told me the closest grocery was over a mile from the project.

Chuck gripped Herb's hand in a firm handshake and, giving me a fatherly hug, he said, "It is hard to say goodbye to all you young people that are going home or to new homes like you two. Since the war ended, I have had to say goodbye to so many of you who have become such good friends. This town has shrunk and the businesses are already feeling the loss. God bless you, and if you ever get back here, be sure to stop by."

We had everything packed except for the few kitchen things we would need in the morning. Early January 1st, we packed everything into the pickup, including a second-hand bed that Herb got talked into buying from our landlord. He got cheated. After Herb had loaded the box springs and mattress on top and tied them down securely, with Mrs. Nelson lending us a hand, she again cautioned Herb about the brakes. I hugged her and thanked her for everything she had done for us while we had lived there. I knew we would never meet again.

Herb was to drive me to Upland, unpack the truck, drive it back, and then hitchhike back to Upland. Neither of us had seen the inside of the apartment, and we had no idea in what condition we would find it.

About a mile from the project, the car in front of us stopped suddenly. Herb pumped the breaks, but the truck didn't stop; we rear-ended that car. It wasn't damaged, but the truck was. Herb pulled into a nearby garage and was told it was a fifty-dollar repair job, but it would be okay to drive on to the project, unload and then drive back to Corona. Herb called Mrs. Nelson and explained what had happened. "Where would you like me to take it for repairs?" he asked. He assured her he would pay for the repairs. There went $50.00 we had counted on for living expenses.

Mrs. Nelson was very understanding and told him where to take the truck. "I will call and tell them to expect you. Don't worry about it. They will return it to me when they have repaired it. I was afraid of those brakes. Don't blame yourself. I am just glad neither of you was hurt."

Herb pulled the truck up to the front door of our apartment, unlocked it, and we went inside to inspect our new home. I was pleasantly surprised. It was a very nice-size two-bedroom with a living room large enough for the furniture we would have to fill it. All the floors were covered with reddish-brown asphalt tiles. The kitchen was adequate and had a dining area at one side. At least the kitchen was not as dirty as I had expected after our experience in Corona.

The paint throughout was good except for some children's marking on a couple of the walls. I would still have to wash them all down and wash the draperies because the former tenants had been smokers and the place reeked of stale smoke.

The ice chest, food, and boxes of dishes and cooking utensils were placed in the kitchen. Everything else ended up in the living room. We hadn't met a soul. We saw people go in and out of their homes, but no one spoke to us or even seemed aware that we were moving in. How different this was from our experience in Corona. Suddenly a wave of loneliness came over me. How I missed my Navy family. I didn't mention it to Herb. He was such happy civilian.

CHAPTER 38

Transition To Civilian Life Was Rough

While Herb took the truck for repairs, I put the perishable food in the icebox and started cleaning the kitchen cupboards and putting things away. I scrubbed the kitchen floor before moving to our bedroom where I proceeded to scrub the floors and clean the closet shelves. By the time he returned, the bedroom was clean and I had hung our clothes in the closet. Together we moved the bed in, set it up and then moved all the boxes from the living room into the bedroom. With the living room empty, it would be easier to clean, ready for our new second-hand furniture to be delivered in the morning.

When we had completed this task, Herb looked at me with concern showing in his face. Taking me in his arms, he asked, "Have you rested at all since I left with the truck?"

"I guess I was so anxious to get everything done that I didn't want to stop," I said, smiling at him. "The furniture we ordered for the living room will be here in the morning, and I want to be ready for it."

Still holding me in his arms, he kissed me and said, "You go in there and lie down. I will scrub the rest of the floors. You have done way too much with all that lifting and scrubbing. Besides, it is almost dinnertime and you know I can't cook," he teased.

I didn't realize how tired I was. The minute my head I hit the pillow, I went to sleep, and did not awaken for over an hour. When I arose, it was dusk. I went out to find Herb had scrubbed all the floors, cleaned the markings off the walls and had set up our card table in the dining area. It was set ready for dinner, and he was sitting, there reading a paper.

As I approached, he laid his paper aside and stood, smiling at me. "You look better, Honey. I was worried, you looked so tired. We don't have to get everything done in one day you know."

I walked into his arms, kissed him and said, "Sorry, honey, but you married a workaholic. I can't rest until things are somewhat in order. I have to be ready for Captain's Inspection, you know. You notice I did get out of scrubbing the rest of the floors. I sure picked the right guy to marry, even if he can't cook. If you let go of me, I will see what I can scrounge up for dinner."

Laughing, he kissed me and said, "Fix something easy, then after dinner and our walk, I will beat you at a game of cards. I'll even help do the dishes.

"By the way, while you were sleeping, I met our neighbors in the other end of this duplex. The husband is an Army vet who is confined to a wheelchair, paralyzed from the waist down. In spite of that, he has a great attitude. He is going to school on the GI Bill, studying to be a jeweler. His wife said hello and excused herself as Ray and I talked on his porch. He watched her go into the house, shook his head, and said, 'This is harder on Mary than on me. I am so glad to be home, I can accept my fate. She said goodbye to a strong, healthy guy, and stayed here with our two boys, and I came home like this. She never complains, but she has lost so much weight and her skin has broken out all over. The doctor said it was from nerves and it will clear up once we are settled. She is embarrassed about it, though, and avoids people. It will be good to have you and your wife next door. She needs to have someone to talk to who understands.'"

"I told him when we got settled in, you would call on her. She needs a friend. You don't mind, do you? I figured, having taken care of all those mangled Sailors and Marines, you would know what to say or not say."

A picture of all those broken bodies flashed before me. I had been able to talk to them and I prayed I would know what to say to the silent, almost forgotten victim, the grieving wife. I said, "You know I will be glad to. Maybe on our walk, if they are on the porch, I can meet them. That will make it easier to call on her later."

After dinner, we put the dishes in the sink and stepped out into the courtyard. It was a warm evening for January. A lady in a nurse's uniform stepped out of her door in the adjoining duplex. We introduced ourselves and she rushed off to her job on the night shift at the hospital. We continued down past the end of the duplex. No one was on the porch, so we walked on.

When we returned, our neighbors were sitting on the porch and Herb led me over to meet them. We talked for a little while and then I said, "If you two ever need anything, we are right next door. Just call." Mary's face lit up. Smiling, she took my hand and thanked me as we bid them goodnight and headed home.

Early the next morning, Herb got up and put on his ROTC Army "Pinks." When I looked surprised, he smiled and said, "No one passes up a veteran, and I can't wear my bellbottoms. They will figure I am an Army vet. It is seven miles from here to the Claremont Men's College, and I hope I don't have to walk it. I have to be back here by four for my Recreation Director's job. That will take an hour and a half to two hours. Since it is my first day, I don't know what to expect. Be sure to check the mailbox. I should be getting a check from the government. I have a feeling the college would like to share it with me." He grinned, kissed me goodbye and was out the door.

Fortunately, our drapes were all washable. There was no washing machine, just a concrete washtub on the back porch. I put the drapes to soak while I washed light fixtures. I used a plunger to wash the drapes. They had to be washed several times to get them clean and to remove the smoke odor. I had just hung them on the line when the truck with the furniture arrived.

Our furniture, which we had purchased at a second-hand store, consisted of a dresser, a couch that opened into a bed, with a lounge chair to match, and a baby bed that was like new. From a local furniture store, I had ordered a new mattress for the crib, along with a kitchen table with four chairs. The table came in a box and had to be assembled, but the price was right.

The driver placed the furniture where I indicated and opened the box containing the unassembled table. Fortunately, it was easy to put together. It had two hinged drop-leaves, but was light enough that, after putting the legs on, I was able to set it up in the dining area in place of the card table. The card table and chairs were moved to the corner of the living room under the windows.

I set apple boxes at each end of the couch to act as end-tables, and placed my one lamp on one and the radio on the other. I would paint them later when I could get the paint.

After a quick lunch and a short nap, I washed the windows, ironed the drapes, and was hanging them when Herb came in. He kissed me and, shaking his head, he said, "You are amazing. This place is beginning to look like a home, but I'll bet you didn't rest."

"Yes I did, and I got the mail. Your check came. How was school? Do you like it?"

"Yes, I like my Advisor and I got my classes set up. I sure am glad to see that check, though." He helped me finish hanging the drapes and then changed into his University of Maryland sweats, kissed me goodbye, and as he went out the door he called back, "See you at six."

Herb returned right at six, gave me a kiss, looked at the dinner I was dishing up and said, "I am starving," as he rushed by to wash up.

While we ate, we discussed his new job. "I don't see how they can afford an Athletic Director here. When I came up in October, there were twenty-five or thirty kids on the field. There was maybe half that number today. The Project Manager said that, since the war ended and fathers were discharged, they had taken their families back to their homes in other areas of the country. Those moving in now are young veterans with either no children or very young children. Most of them are going back to school or searching for jobs. I am keeping my eyes open for something else, in case this falls apart. Thank God for the GI Bill."

CHAPTER 39

Apple Boxes and Orange Crates

After seeing Herb off to school, I walked into town to keep an appointment with my new doctor. Our doctor in Corona had referred me to an old friend of his and had made this appointment for me.

When I arrived, I was informed that the doctor to whom I had been referred had had a heart attack and I had been scheduled to see a much younger doctor who had been hired to fill in for him.

I had misgivings. I would have preferred an older doctor with more years of experience. I was taken into the examining room and, as I waited, I observed frames on the wall, one containing a diploma issued only two years earlier and one recognizing the doctor for his time in the Service. I wanted to run out of there. Had he had any experience delivering babies? Where would I go? My baby was due the 18th of March, we had no car, and I knew no one in this town to ask for a referral to another doctor. The door opened and the young doctor walked in, carrying my chart. I was trapped.

After examining me, he said, "Well, in a couple months you should have a nice, healthy six- or seven-pound baby." That is what my Corona doctor had told me, so when I left his office I was feeling a little better.

I found a hardware store where I picked up a couple of curtain rods, some nails, a hammer, small saw, and sandpaper. As I headed for the paint department, I passed a rack of shelf paper. One caught my eye, a heavy glue-down type with a wood-grain pattern that should work better than paint on the apple boxes. I added several rolls to my basket and headed on to the paint department where I chose a very light blue paint, a can of primer and some brushes.

From there I went to a yardage store and was able to find remnants of material, a pale yellow with little white lambs all over it. This would work for curtains in the baby's room.

My next stop was the grocery store where I bought the few groceries I needed. Loaded down with all my purchases, I started the long walk home. Once I left the business area, there was no place to stop to rest. I would walk for a while, stop, and switch the bags from one hand to the other, repeating this several times before I arrived home.

After a short rest, I covered five apple boxes, inside and out, with the shelf paper. With a doily on top, if you didn't inspect too closely, they looked like finished wood. I placed one at each end of the couch, one beside the chair and one on each side of our bed. The paper cost a little more than paint but I felt it made the end-tables looked nicer.

I took the orange crates out on the porch. After setting two of them on end, side by side, I could see what I needed to do to create storage for the baby's room.

I removed the slats, one at a time, sanding and replacing them closely together on one side of the crate. I repeated this on the back and removed the slats from the third side. I repeated this on the second crate and stood them side by side, with the open sides together. The ends of the boxes were solid.

To stabilize them and hold the crates together, I took some of the slats, cut them to fit, sanded the ends, placed them over the breaks where the crates came together, and tacked them in place. Since I would be turning the boxes over, I needed to place a slat at each end so it would sit level. That accomplished, I turned the crates face down and completed tacking the rest of the slats to close the back.

When finished, I stood my creation right side up and stood back to admire it. Painting would be tomorrow's project, along with making a little curtain for the front of the two shelves.

I had been so busy that I didn't hear Herb come in the back door and through the house. He opened the door, startling me. I was covered with sawdust. Kissing me, he said, "What are you up to now?"

Grinning at him, I said, "I decided to go into the furniture business. This dresser, curtains for the baby's room, and our end-tables cost you less than ten dollars, including the tools I had to buy. Cost of design and labor is another thing. You arrived just in time. You can help me move these things inside so they won't get wet from the night air. Right now, I had better get cleaned up and start dinner."

"Woman, you never cease to amaze me. I saw what you did to the apple boxes. Did you rest today?" he asked, as he carried my creation inside.

"After that walk to town and carrying all my purchases home, you bet I did," I said, laughing at his concern.

Before leaving for school the following day, Herb took everything back out on the porch for me. I left the dishes on the table, took my paint out, and gave everything a coat of primer before cleaning up the kitchen. When I returned to the porch, the primer had dried, ready for painting. I was pleased with the finished product and went in to work on the curtains while the paint dried.

After measuring and cutting the material to make curtains for the window and new dresser, I set up the sewing table, placed my little Singer in it, and in no time my curtains were ready to thread onto the curtain rods. I climbed up onto a chair, nailed in the little brackets that had come with the rods and hung the window curtains.

I decided to take a break and visit Mary before lunch. If she was home, she didn't answer the door. I was concerned because I knew she was deeply depressed.

By the time Herb got home from the ball field, the paint was dry on the little dresser and I had attached the brackets for the curtain. "I said, Herb, dinner is in the oven, but before we eat, would you help me move our new dresser in?" Together we carefully took it into the baby's room, set it across from the baby bed, and I hung the curtain on the front.

We stepped back, admiring the finished room. I felt his arm slip over my shoulder as he walked me through the house. He pulled me close and said, "This place looks great. I can't believe how you have transformed it. That was the best almost-ten dollars I ever spent. I sure got a bargain on the product. Now what do I owe you for design and labor?"

I laughed, "Don't worry, I will think of something, but right now I had better take your dinner out of the oven before it burns."

CHAPTER 40

52/20

After two weeks at the Project, Herb announced that he had been told he would no longer have a job there. There weren't enough children to warrant the expense. "I have been looking for something else, anticipating this. I am going tomorrow at four AM to pick up golf balls at the local club. I will give it a try while I watch for something better. During the week, I will have to go right from the club to school. It doesn't pay much, but we need the money."

He hesitated for a few minutes and said, "Ruth, I know how you feel about taking money that you don't feel you have earned, but I believe you should think about signing up for the 52/20 program. It isn't charity any more than the GI Bill money. It was set up to help veterans while they are trying to transition back into civilian life. You are required to sign up and appear once a week, ready to take a job if offered, but only if it is a job equal to the one you had when you enlisted. As long as you appear once a week, you receive $20 for 52 weeks unless you find a job."

"I know, Herb, but who in their right mind would hire a lady who is seven months pregnant? Even if there was someone who would hire me, I was an apprentice pharmacist in my last job.

Those jobs don't exist anymore. If they offered me any job I could do, I would feel obligated to take it, whatever it was. When our baby arrives, I would have to quit. That seems unfair to the employer." Seeing the worried look on his face, I added, "I will think about it, though."

Herb worked Saturday and was hired. Monday morning, he arose at 3:30, ate a bowl of cold cereal, and rushed to the golf course while I slept. I felt so guilty that after breakfast I walked to town and signed up for the 52/20 program.

When I filled out the application, I didn't bother to list Apprentice Pharmacist. Instead, I listed "Clerked in a drugstore and managed the cosmetic department and soda fountain."

The gentleman in charge scanned my application, searched through their short list of available jobs, and said, "I am very sorry, Mrs. Gunther, but there is nothing here for you. I am required to match the jobs to your qualifications, and you are overqualified for any of the jobs available." He handed me a check for twenty dollars and told me to come back in a week. "Maybe something will show up by that time," he said.

I felt the heat rise in my face as I thanked him and walked out, carrying the check. As I left, I thought to myself, "What would my father say?" I could see his face and hear his words in the depths of the depression, "As long as I can work, my family will not accept charity." That check seemed to burn my fingers.

Leaving the Government Employment Office, I walked a short distance to the grocery and headed for the meat counter to find the cases nearly empty. There were rabbits displayed, but no chicken, bacon, pork, lamb or beef. "What is going on?" I asked the butcher. "Where is all the meat?"

He shook his head sympathetically and said, "The farmers are holding their meat off the market, trying to kill the price control that was put on during the war and has never been removed. They can't afford to raise their animals and get them to market for the prices the government has set. It will be a while before you will see pork, beef or lamb in the case."

I bought a rabbit and went to the canned-food department where I picked up several cans of Spam, tuna, and dried beef, along with dried beans. I heard shoppers complaining that the butcher kept what meat they did get for their faithful old customers who had been with them for years. I thought of Chuck.

As I approached the checkout, I blushed when I handed the government check to the clerk, and was relieved to get it out of my hand.

Every week thereafter I made that dreaded trip and received the same answer, "Sorry, Mrs. Gunther, there are no jobs for which you qualify." I would walk out with a check and stop at the grocery to cash it. I continued to check the meat counter with the same results. We were getting very tired of rabbit and Spam.

February arrived, but our GI check didn't. Herb contacted the government and was told it had been mailed. They would put a tracer on it. They were sorry, but they couldn't issue another check to us until they found the missing one. I realized now how important that 52/20 check was. We had saved money for the hospital and doctor, and that would not be touched.

One Sunday, about the middle of February, Rose and Vern West showed up and surprised us. We hadn't seen them since the wedding. Rose brought everything already cooked for our dinner, and we spent the day reminiscing. Vern had kept in touch with everyone and he filled us in on what was going on in their lives. We hated to see them leave.

The following week, I went in to the Government Office, received the same, "No work available," picked up my check, and left. As I turned toward the grocery, I passed a store with a baby carriage displayed in the window. It was on sale for $19.95. I stopped and stood there, thinking, "Do I have enough food in my cupboards that I dare buy that carriage?" I knew I would not be able to walk to town for groceries and carry them and a baby home. I decided I could make what food I had stretch for a week. I walked in, bought the carriage and pushed it home.

Herb came home tired. He kissed me and went to wash before dinner. I waited until after dinner and the dishes were done before I said, "Come see what I bought today." I led him into the baby's room and showed him the carriage.

He looked at me unsmiling and asked quietly, "How much did you pay for that? You know we can't afford anything that we don't really need. We don't need that."

My joy turned to anger and I said, "Herb, I enjoyed making furniture out of boxes; I am happy with second-hand furniture; I have not complained about sleeping on a worn-out mattress with the springs poking me every time I move, and I can make a dollar stretch farther than anyone you know, but I am not a horse. In a month, I will have a baby. How do you expect me to carry a baby over a mile to town and back with my groceries? That baby buggy may not be a necessity to you, but it is to me. You think about it. I am going for a walk." I left him standing there and turned to leave before he saw the tears rolling down my cheeks.

Herb caught my arm before I could reach the kitchen door. Forcing me to face him, he said, "I am sorry, honey. I spoke before I thought. We do need that buggy. I guess I can't help worrying about money, even though you have managed so well on so little and we have never gone hungry." He held me close, wiped away my tears, and whispered, "Am I forgiven?"

March came, still no check, and Herb received the same story from the government. Herb went to see his counselor at the college and explained what had happened. They agreed to work with him by allowing him to finish his schooling. He signed a note with his GI money as collateral, promising to pay when his school money came in. If he got a job before the money arrived, he would pay back the loan on an installment plan until his debt was paid. We were both relieved and amazed at their understanding and generosity. My weekly $20 and Herb's golf club job paid the rent and fed us, but there was no money for anything extra. It was a good thing we enjoyed each other's company.

CHAPTER 41

Our Son Arrives

March eleventh, I put a large pot of beans to soak before heading to town for my check and groceries. That would be an easy dinner tonight and Herb would have leftovers if and when my time came.

Shortly after dinner, I was hit with excruciating pains, one on top of the other. They were nothing like I had expected. I had been told to go into the hospital when the pains were one minute apart, but they never were a minute apart. I thought to myself, "If only I had an experienced friend nearby that I could call on," but I didn't.

Herb looked frightened to death, and I shared his fear. I said, "You had better call a cab and get me to the hospital, Herb. He flew out of the door and was back within five minutes; the cab arrived shortly thereafter.

Twenty-seven hours after we reached the hospital, our son John Stephen was born, weighing in at nine pounds and measuring twenty-one-and-a-half inches. I was moved into a room and Herb was allowed in. They had taken the baby to prepare him for viewing. Herb would have to look at him through the glass of the Nursery.

Herb sat down beside me, gathered me in his arms, hugged me, and buried his face in my shoulder. "I thought I was going to lose you," he sobbed. "I couldn't have gone on if I had. You are my life. Never again! I can't see you suffer like that ever again!"

We clung to each other and I cried with him. "Everyone says the first child is always the hardest," I said. "Wait until you see your son. You will change your mind. The nurses told me you stayed with me all the time; you must be tired. I am fine now. Why don't you go to the Nursery, see your son and then go home and rest? The nurses say he looks like a six-month-old and has fists like a boxer."

This brought a smile to his face. "I do want to see our son," and then, laughing, he added, "and I am tired after having that baby. I think I will take your advice. I will be back tonight, Honey. You get some rest." He hugged me and left, only to return in about twenty minutes to tell me about our son. "He is the biggest and the best looking baby in the Nursery. Even the nurses tell me that," he said, beaming with pride.

After Herb left, a nurse came in and set up an IV. She said. "You lost a lot of blood in the Delivery Room and the doctor has ordered two pints to replace it. You should feel much stronger after this."

I was told I would be in the hospital two weeks, and Herb came every evening and weekends to visit me. Each time, he stopped by the Nursery to admire his son.

Watching the nurses and aides working, I was shocked at the lack of training and sterile technique used in that hospital. I could not help comparing it with the care and sterile technique patients received in the Navy Hospital. I could hardly wait to be released and take my baby home.

The day I brought John home from the hospital, I removed his wet diaper and was horrified. He was covered with sores I believed to be impetigo, and the umbilical cord had dropped off before the skin had grown together. I was both horrified and angry. This was from lack of care and unsanitary conditions in the Nursery.

I remembered the nurse next door whom we had met shortly after we moved in. We hadn't seen her since, but I ran across the yard and knocked on her door. Fortunately, it was her day off and she followed me back into my house and into the nursery. Johnny still lay there uncovered. I was most worried about the open navel.

She looked at him and said, "You are right. He has impetigo. The navel will heal over soon. Just keep him dry. We are so short-staffed at the hospital that babies don't get changed as often as they should, and these things happen." I thanked her and she left.

I dressed Johnny, bundled him up, laid him in his buggy and headed to the public phone. I called the doctor and told him my baby was covered with impetigo.

His response was, "Well that doesn't surprise me. They have been having trouble in the Nursery with this. Sterilize a needle, open all the blisters and clean them with alcohol. You must boil every piece of clothing and bedding that touches him to avoid this spreading." I did as he said, and John screamed every time I changed him.

From the time we brought him home, John cried most of the night and much of the day. I nursed him frequently, but he never seemed satisfied. I determined they must have been giving him supplemental feedings at the hospital.

After a week with almost no sleep, I took him into the doctor. "There is something wrong with my baby," I said. "He cries constantly. When I nurse him, he never seems satisfied. I don't think he is getting enough to eat. Couldn't I try supplementing his feedings with a formula?" I asked.

He was examining John as I spoke. "There is nothing wrong with this baby. You modern mothers just don't want to bother to nurse your babies. I will not recommend a formula. Just give it more time." I wanted to tell him what a lousy doctor he was, but I bit my tongue.

After another week with a crying baby and little sleep, I made a decision. I nursed John, changed him, and placed him in the buggy, and we walked to the Project Office. I found the public phone and searched through the Yellow Pages for a pediatrician. There was one in Ontario. I jotted down the address and, pushing the buggy, I walked to town where I caught a bus to Ontario.

Finding the doctor's office, I walked in without an appointment. Fortunately, it was early in the morning and her morning appointments had not yet arrived. The nurse checked with the doctor and took me right in. By this time, John was crying at the top of his lungs. I told her everything from the day I went to the hospital up to and including my last visit with the doctor and what he had said.

After examining John, she said, "This baby is starving. He is too big for you to try to feed without a supplement." She called her nurse and instructed her to fill a bottle with formula and give it to me. Then, turning to me, she said, "You stop trying to nurse this baby immediately and don't let anyone make you feel guilty about it," she ordered.

I took the bottle of warm formula from the nurse, offered it to John, and watched my poor starving baby devour it.

The doctor smiled and said, "You are to feed this baby every two hours, day and night: Set your clock. If he goes to sleep before he finishes his bottle, thump him on the bottom of his foot with your thumb and forefinger to keep him awake. Do this for two weeks and then bring him back to see me. Here, take the rest of this can of formula. You can buy more at drugstores or grocery stores. I am giving you instructions on how to prepare it. If the formula doesn't agree with him, call me immediately and I will give you a different one."

Seeing my concerned look, she said, smiling, "Don't worry. If you follow my instructions, your baby will be fine and so will you. Call me any time if you have questions." She started to turn to leave, put an arm over my shoulder and added, "Since you had the good sense to seek help for your baby, maybe you should consider doing the same for yourself. There is a very good doctor down the hall. You relax and I will see you in two weeks." Smiling, she patted me on the shoulder and left.

As I left the office, I looked down at my sleeping baby and thanked God for leading me through the Yellow Pages to this doctor.

I caught the first bus to Upland. John was sleeping soundly in his buggy as I entered the grocery store, picked up several cans of formula and a few groceries, placed them in the end of the buggy and headed home.

By the time I had sterilized his bottles and filled several of them with formula, it was time to waken the soundly sleeping baby and feed him. For the first time since I had brought him home from the hospital, he had slept two full hours, and now he didn't want to be wakened. After feeding and changing him, I laid him in his bed and set the alarm for two hours.

It was after noon, but I was too tired to bother with lunch; instead, I lay down for a few minutes. Two hours later, I was startled out of a sound sleep by the alarm clock. I jumped up and ran to the baby's room, thinking that loud alarm would have frightened him. He was lying in the same position I had placed him. I couldn't see him breathing and thought he was dead. Snatching him up, I held him close. I felt panic take over and then I felt his warm face against mine and felt him move. Dropping into the closest chair, I clung to my baby and, sobbing with relief, I thanked God. My baby was still sound asleep. It was the first time he had had enough to eat since I had brought him home from the hospital. He was finally satisfied.

With two-hour feedings, it was difficult to get anything else done. I struggled to keep John awake while feeding him. That poor little foot got thumped a lot. I felt as if I would never be rested, but my baby was happy. After two weeks of this schedule, I took him back to the doctor.

She was pleased with his progress and said, "I am going to increase the amount of formula for each feeding, and you can now start feeding him every three hours during the day and whenever he is hungry at night. If he isn't satisfied, increase the amount of formula by one ounce. Come back to see me in one month. Be sure to call if you have any questions or problems." John was six weeks old now and a healthy, happy baby.

CHAPTER 42

Our Wonderful New Friends

*I*t was April first, and no check came. Herb made the same calls with the same answer. It had been only four months since Herb was discharged, but so much had happened in that four months, it seemed much longer. I thought to myself, "Do all veterans go through what we have gone through? Are any of them getting their GI money?"

The following day, when he returned from school, Herb said, "Ruth, we have new neighbors across the courtyard, Paul and Elenita White. They have a little girl, Stephanie, about eighteen months old. Paul is an Air Force veteran and is going to Claremont for his teaching credential. He wants to coach in a high school. We have a lot in common: We are both veterans, love sports and have played a lot of ball. He works for an elderly lady in her citrus groves in Ontario. I rode home with Paul and met his wife. You will like her."

I was excited at the thought of a neighbor with something in common. I had tried to befriend Mary, but when I stopped by, she never answered the door, and I determined she didn't want a friend. On our evening walks, if we saw them on their porch, we stopped to visit for a few minutes and they seemed to appreciate it, but they never reciprocated and I gave up.

Herb continued, "Paul invited us to come over after they get their little girl fed and put to bed, any time after seven. We can take John in the buggy, since he is sleeping so well now."

A little after seven, we took that walk across the courtyard with our baby to what was the beginning of a lifelong friendship. To me, they were a couple of God's angels. We had so much in common and I desperately needed a friend.

'Do you play poker?" Paul asked. "We can't afford to play for money. We use toothpicks or kitchen matches instead." That last statement was a relief, since our April check had not come and I no longer got the $20 a week. We couldn't even afford pennies, and neither could our new friends.

We hadn't done anything socially since my discharge seven months earlier, and I felt my loneliness lift. Herb won most of Paul's matches and he took it as if they had been silver dollars. Coaches don't like to lose. We exchanged stories of our experiences, teased each other, joked, and laughed together until about nine thirty when Johnny let us know it was feeding time. From that day on, we wore a path across that courtyard, playing poker or just visiting.

Paul, Elenita, and their daughter Stephanie

In May, I received a telegram from my older brother, Raymond. It read, "Grandpa killed last night by speeding car, letter to follow." I heard an unearthly scream that seemed to come from the depths of my soul and I realized it had come from me. I fell onto the couch and sobbed. I couldn't imagine life without Grandpa. He had always been there for his grandchildren and it had never occurred to me that that would change. It would have been easier had he died from natural causes, but to be killed by a speeding car! I just couldn't accept it. As I lay there, sobbing, I thought, "What more can happen to us?" Several days later, the letter came, explaining what had happened. It didn't relieve my pain.

One evening, Paul came over. Walking into the kitchen, he said, "I have a job for you, Herb. They are predicting two or three nights of freezing weather, and I have to line up workers to keep the smudge pots going in the orchards so the oranges don't freeze. It is dirty work and it may be an all-night job, but it pays pretty well. Would you be interested?"

Herb smiled and said, "I will do anything. Just tell me where, when, and what to do, and I will be there."

Paul laughed, "You had better get some sleep now because you will be working until the temperature in the grove rises enough that we don't have to worry. I am watching the temperature, and when it drops to a dangerous level, I will be over to pick you up. I hope you have some old clothes to wear because you will look like a smudge pot when you return." Turning to me, he said, "Ruth, be sure to keep all the windows closed tight. When we smudge, that black oily smoke doesn't stay in the orchard; it is picked up by the wind and you will find an oily black film over everything.

Herb grinned, "Old clothes, I don't think that will be a problem for me." They both chuckled. "I really appreciate you thinking of me, Paul. I will sleep in my clothes so I won't hold you up."

Around eleven, we were awakened by a knock on the door. Herb grabbed his shoes and left. It was very early in the morning when he returned. The only white skin I saw was the band across his forehead that the band of his baseball cap had covered. Dropping his oily clothes in the kitchen, he went into the bathroom to scrub from head to toe. I gathered up his clothes and put them to soak in the washtub. He would need them again tonight.

While Herb bathed and dressed, I fixed breakfast and packed his lunch. He ate quickly, grabbed the lunch and hurriedly kissed me as he rushed off to pick up golf balls before going to school. Over dinner he told me about smudging trees. It was a dirty job, but we were so thankful for the money. His clothes had been scrubbed clean and were ready for him to wear when Paul came for him that night.

Months went by with no government check. Our debt to the college was growing. We didn't know it then, but the government money would not catch up with us for another five months and most of that would go to the college to pay our debt.

In late September, Herb's Advisor approached him and said, "Herb, there is a job opening in Banning that I believe you could have if you want it. All you need now is your practice teaching, and I would be willing to drive up there a few times to observe your teaching and give you the college credit you need. It is only about fifty miles from here.

Herb came home walking on air. He picked me up and swung me in a circle. "Your husband is going to Banning for an interview. I may have a job coaching and teaching. My Advisor has recommended me and made an appointment with the Superintendent for tomorrow. I will hitchhike up in the morning and will be back tomorrow night for dinner." He was dancing me around the room to the big band music that played on my radio.

Early the next morning, Herb went to pick up golf balls. When he returned, I fixed him a big breakfast, and before he left for his interview, we held each other and prayed that he would get the job and come home safely. With no phone, I would just have to wait until he returned that night to see if he was hired.

It was almost six in the evening when Herb walked into the nursery where I had just put our sleeping baby in bed. Herb slipped his arms around me and kissed me. "I have missed you two," he said, smiling, as we stood looking down at our sleeping son.

We walked out into the living room. Since Herb hadn't mentioned his interview, I was afraid to ask. I looked at his expressionless face and my heart sank. I just stood there looking at him and I finally said, "Well, is it good news or bad news?"

He laughed, "I thought you would never ask. Mrs. Gunther, your husband is the new Assistant Coach at The Banning Union High School, coaching baseball, football, basketball and tennis. I will also be teaching five subjects, Physics, Algebra, Physical Education, General Science and Mechanical Drawing. I will be making eighteen hundred a year, which will be paid over a ten month period."

I threw myself at him, hugging him with joy and excitement. "Herb, I am so proud of you and so happy we will now have a regular income we can depend on, but I can't imagine how anyone can coach four sports and teach five different subjects. Coaching will take all your time after school. When will you have time to prepare for that many classes?"

"I know it won't be easy, but that was the job they offered me," he said. "I was afraid to try to bargain with them. I need a job. I want to be able to take care of my family and pay off my college debt. The only thing that worries me is Physics. I haven't had Physics since high school." He was so excited and relieved that I held my misgivings inside.

While we ate, Herb told me about the school. "I really liked Al Zollers, the Head Coach," he said. "I met several of the teachers, and they agreed to watch for a rental for us.

"After meeting with Dr. Peterson and signing my contract, I went to a realtor, but he had nothing to show me. He said no one in Banning would rent to families with children and he would suggest we check Beaumont, which is six miles West of Banning. We might have to live in Beaumont and I will have to hitchhike to work, not the best situation, but even if I have to walk, I can do it.

"Tomorrow I will go in, consult with my Advisor and finalize whatever I need there. I have to report for work October 1st at seven AM. I have found a cheap motel room and have arranged to rent it Sunday night through Thursday night at a special rate. This leaves the weekend open when the owner can rent it for more. I will go up on Sunday evening, stay there through Thursday night, and come home Friday after school while I search for a place for us."

After dinner, we took Johnny and walked across to tell the Whites our good news. Paul brought out a special bottle of Gallo wine to celebrate our good fortune.

Herb had been working in Banning for almost two months with no luck in finding a rental. By the time they took out Social Security, Withholding, and our Retirement contribution, our $180 paycheck had shrunk. It was taking every penny Herb made for us to live in two places. Our rent money and the baby's needs came out first. I managed on very little. Herb kept milk in a small refrigerator in his room and ate cold cereal every morning. He saved by eating his lunch in the school cafeteria, but he had to eat out at night.

When Herb came home on the weekend, we discussed his progress in house-hunting. He said, "I mentioned to the Superintendent that there were rentals in Beaumont, and was told, 'If you want to work in Banning, you had better live in Banning.'"

We were getting desperate. Herb said, "I talked to the Realtor again and he suggested that we think about buying a place. There is a builder who is building three houses two miles west of town. He took me to see one of them that is almost finished. We could buy it on the GI Bill with nothing down, and our payments wouldn't be any more than renting."

"I like the idea of owning our own home. Maybe for once we could move into a home that didn't have to be cleaned before we could live in it. Why don't you check on it more and find out what bank is making GI loans and what we have to do to qualify? I have heard most banks are steering clear of them, since veterans don't have any credit background."

CHAPTER 43

Our Birthday Surprise

Herb's birthday was Wednesday, November 20th and mine was Friday the 22nd. I decided to celebrate both on Friday when Herb got home.

Johnny was down for his nap, and dinner was in the oven. I had made a three-layer chocolate cake and frosted it with a boiled fudge frosting. I was just putting the finishing touches to the frosting when there was a knock on the door. I hurried to open it and couldn't believe my eyes. There stood my mother.

"I wanted to surprise you for your birthday," she said, "and I think I did." We were hugging each other. I could not believe she would have taken the train this far by herself. I was proud of her.

"I wanted to see you and Herb, and that new grandson of mine. I never dreamed I would ever get to California, but here I am. Before Grandpa's death, he brought your last letter over for me to read. After I read it, he said, 'Gladys, I wish I had the money. I would take you to California to see that new grandson of ours.' It wasn't a week later that he was killed. When I received his insurance check, I thought to myself, 'Papa wanted to take me to California. I believe he would have approved of my using some of this money to visit you.'"

Tears welled up in my eyes as I said, "I am sure he would, Mom." After hearing all the news from home, I told her the problems we had had finding a place to live. We were now looking at a place to buy with a GI loan. I repeated what the Realtor had told us. And then I said, "Mom don't you think you should lie down for a while before Herb gets home and the baby wakes up? She assured me she had been able to sleep on the train. "Mom, I remember those long days and nights traveling to and from Indiana and how tired I got."

She gave in and agreed to lie down after I promised to awaken her before Herb got home.

Mom was up the minute John stirred. Lifting him from his crib, I handed him to her. While she played with him, I fixed his bottle and let her feed him.

It was time for Herb to arrive home. I was putting dinner on the table while Mom watched for him through the window. "Here he comes. I want to surprise him," she said, as she stepped out of sight beside the door. I stood facing the door as it opened. He was smiling at me with his hand still on the knob when Mom grabbed his wrist. He whirled and saw her standing there, smiling.

"Mom, where did you come from? What a wonderful surprise!" He hugged her and lifted her off her feet. "You don't know how welcome this visit is. What a great birthday gift you have given us!"

Turning, he kissed me and led me to the living room where John sat playing on a blanket on the floor. John smiled broadly as his little arms shot up and he squealed, "Da-Da."

Herb picked him up and lifted him high over his head to hear him shout with glee, before taking him to the table and setting him in his highchair next to me so I could feed him while we ate.

As we ate, Herb told Mom about his job and his house-hunting experiences, and she filled him in on all the news about the family at home and her train trip through the mountains and desert. While they talked, I got up and warmed John's bottle. Mom watched and then asked, "Would you like me to feed Johnny?"

"That would be great, Mom. When he is fed, you can put him in the buggy. Herb and I will clean up here. We want you to meet our neighbors, Paul and Elenita White. We want to take our cake over to their house to celebrate our birthdays with them. They have been great friends, in fact our only friends since we got out of the Service. I want them to meet you."

When we were finished in the kitchen, I took John, changed him, put him in his sleeper and then in the buggy. Herb held the door as I pushed the buggy out into the courtyard. Herb carried the cake in one hand and offered Mom his arm. "There is no sidewalk across the courtyard and I don't want my mother-in-law to turn her ankle and sue me," he teased. Mom swatted him on the arm, but took it with a smile.

After introductions, Elenita offered coffee for anyone who wanted it, and I cut our cake. As we ate, Herb told everyone about his progress on housing.

"I signed a purchase agreement on that house I told you all about. It is conditioned upon Ruth's approval and the house qualifying for a GI loan. Mr. Stoll said the Bank of America in Redlands is the only bank making GI loans. If Ruth likes the house, he will take her to Redlands to fill out the papers and drop her off at the bus station so she will get home before dark. He will bring the papers I need to sign back up to me. I can drop by the bank Friday on my way home and be sure everything is in order. The builder said we should be able to move in during Christmas vacation."

Elenita offered, "I would be glad to keep Johnny if you want me to."

Mom smiled and said, "Herb, I raised twelve children. I think I can take care of my grandson. We will get along fine. Just leave instructions on feeding and phone numbers where you can be reached. This will give me a chance to get to know Johnny. If you need to stay another day, Ruth, you can call Elenita to let me know. I will be fine. If I have any problems, maybe I could call on you, Elenita."

Elenita smiled and said, "You certainly may. I will run over from time to time and visit you, or you can bring Johnny over in the buggy to visit us. Stephanie loves to play with him. And if you need anything from the store, Paul can pick it up for you on his way home."

I didn't worry about the baby. I knew Mom would love staying with him, and he already loved his Grandma. I fixed an early dinner and we left soon after. Mom wouldn't need to cook. There were plenty of leftovers in the icebox.

When we reached Banning, we contacted Mr. Stoll and met him at the house. He let us in, and when I saw the mess, my heart sank. The drywall had been installed and I don't believe there had ever been any construction cleanup. You couldn't see the floor for scraps of drywall and construction trash.

I looked at our Realtor and he read my mind. "Don't worry, Mrs. Gunther. They will clean this up. They haven't finished yet, but it will be ready for you to move in during Christmas vacation, as you planned." I had my doubts, but I had cleaned before, and I wanted a home.

We stood in a 12'x20' living room. The kitchen was the same size as the bath, and the two bedrooms were 12'x12' each. There was a gas panel heater in the wall, opening both ways between the living room and the hall. This was to heat the entire 700 square feet of house. There was no garage or storage area. Outside the kitchen door was an 8'x8' screened-in porch with a concrete washtub. The house sat on a half acre with nothing growing but tumbleweeds.

I signed the papers and Mr. Stoll dropped us off at the high school so Herb could show me around. As we stepped out of the car, it was agreed that Mr. Stoll would pick me up at the motel at 8:30 the next morning and take me to the bank in Redlands to fill out the necessary papers.

After touring the school grounds, Herb and I wandered through town. It was a beautiful spot, nestled between two snow-capped mountains. At times, the wind blew through that pass 70 miles an hour, bringing with it mountains of prickly tumbleweeds that could pile up as high as your house, dropping their seeds as they tumbled. It was high desert, cold in the winter and hot in the summer.

Herb and I found a little restaurant near the motel, where we ate and talked about the house and what we would need to buy when we moved in. We would be two miles from town and the grocery store. The first thing on our list was an icebox. Factories were slowly converting back to producing household needs such as telephones, refrigerators and washers, but you had to sign up for them and take your turn. Herb had already put our name on a waiting list for all of these things and had been told it might be two years or more before we could get any of them.

After eating, we walked back to the motel. This was the first time I had been away from our son, and it seemed strange. We played cards for a while, but we were both tired from our long day and turned in early. It was difficult getting any sleep. There seemed to be no end to the trains that went through that pass.

We went out for breakfast, after which Herb walked me back to the motel and then hiked up the hill to the school. Mr. Stoll arrived promptly at eight-thirty and we were in the bank by nine. It seemed to take forever to fill out all the forms, sign all the documents, and finally get on the bus. The bus stopped about a half mile from home; I got off and hiked up the hill.

When I walked into the kitchen, Mom greeted me and said she had food warming for our dinner. "You go check on your boy. He was so good while you were gone."

I slipped into John's room. He was playing happily in his bed until he saw me. "Mama, Mama," his arms shot up and he started to cry. I picked him up and he grabbed me around the neck, hanging on for dear life. He wouldn't let me put him in his highchair, so I held him while we ate.

Mom laughed and said, "He was fine until you got here."

Paul was going to pick up a roasting hen for their Thanksgiving dinner from a farmer he knew, and offered to pick up one for us. I thanked him and gave him money. Thursday, November 28th, would be Thanksgiving, the first one I had spent with Mom since 1942. Herb would get home on Wednesday evening and have until Sunday to visit with Mom before she had to leave.

While Herb took his son for a walk around the Project, Mom and I worked together creating a Thanksgiving feast which included her famous pumpkin pie. It was like old times except that Grandpa would not be with us to say grace. It was good that Mom was spending the day with us.

Mom spoke up. "This is the first Thanksgiving I have ever been away from home. All your sisters and brothers and their families, except Mabel, are at Arthur's for Thanksgiving dinner right now. Herb, I hope someday you can come back and be there with us."

Monday, we started packing. I turned my end-tables on their backs and carefully packed all my cookware, dishes and glassware, holding back only what we needed. Paul brought me several cardboard boxes for the rest of our things and volunteered to move us in his truck.

Herb came home Friday, the 12th of December. Mom was to leave Sunday the 14th. I hated to think of her leaving. I had taken advantage of those three weeks together. I was able to get most of our belongings packed while we talked. She loved taking care of Johnny and we visited while taking our daily walk around the Project, pushing him in his buggy.

I caught the bus to Redlands one day to sign final papers on the house, leaving Mom in charge of Johnny. He was happy as a clam. He knew his Grandma by now.

Herb came home Friday, December 13th, and announced, "Our loan has been approved and the house is ours, but Mr. Stoll said the government had appraised the house for six thousand and the builder wanted sixty-five hundred. He said we will have to pay him that five hundred apart from escrow, or he won't go through with the deal."

We were so naive, we didn't know that the seller could not demand more than the appraised value, but the Realtor had to have known and should not have let us sign loan documents until it was settled. I was in shock.

"Herb, what can we do? We have signed loan documents and I understood the house had been transferred to our name. There is no way we can buy that house. We can't come up with $500. We owe the college $400. If the GI money would arrive, we could do it, but who knows when that will happen?"

Herb said, "I know, Ruth, but I think we are obligated since we signed everything. It is strange that Stoll didn't tell us this before everything was signed. Paul has scheduled his work so he can move us the 28th."

Seeing our distress, Mom spoke up. "I have my insurance money in the bank and it isn't drawing much interest there. Let me loan you the five hundred." Herb and I looked at her and then at each other. We were shocked. We knew she had never had money in savings, and here she was offering to loan us money. God works in mysterious ways. I hated to think that Grandpa's death had made it possible for us to buy our house.

We both objected, but she insisted. "If it makes you feel better, you can pay me the interest I am earning in the bank," she said.

I said, "Mom, the only way we will borrow from you is if you let us pay you the same interest as we will be paying on the house loan: that is, four percent."

Mom smiled, "That is much better than I could get anywhere else," she said.

On Sunday, we had a special early dinner for Mom. Herb said, "Mom, I am going to take the bus with you as far as San Bernardino, and then I will hitch a ride on to Banning. It will give us some time together and I can see you safely onto the train." Mom beamed her approval, "You will be taking the same train Ruth and I took when we went back to see you after we were married. That train travels through the center of the town of Banning, so you will be able to see it. It is a beautiful town."

Herb called a cab, and after saying our goodbyes, Johnny and I stood watching and waving until it was out of sight. I was so thankful for the time we had had together with Mom and for her generous offer. Things seemed to be looking up for us at last, but I could not help wondering when Mom and I would see each other again.

CHAPTER 44

Our Move To Our New Home

Christmas Day, we laid a blanket on the floor of the living room and we placed the few unwrapped toys we had bought for Johnny in a circle. Herb took him from me and set him in the center. John sat looking from one to the other saying, "Oh! Oh!" over and over as he reached for them one at a time. We stuck to our agreement this Christmas, that we would not give each other gifts. The gifts for our baby were enough for us.

The following day, Herb and I packed all our belongings except for our beds and what we would need the next morning. Elenita fixed dinner for us and we spent our last evening together. We would miss these wonderful friends, but swore we would keep in touch.

December 27th, Herb and I arose early and ate breakfast, and while Paul and Herb loaded everything into the truck, I awakened Johnny and fed and dressed him warmly, ready for the cold weather in Banning. He was nine months old now and such a happy, contented baby. We left the keys in the house, closed the door, and, after hugging Elenita and Stephie goodbye, I climbed into the truck, next to Paul. Herb handed me the baby and climbed in after us.

We laughed and joked as the truck climbed the mountain. The higher we climbed, the colder it got. When we arrived at our new home, the wind must have been blowing sixty miles per hour off those snow-capped mountains on either side of the San Gorgonio Pass. Mr. Stoll was there to meet us with our keys. He unlocked the door, and as I entered, carrying Johnny, I looked around in dismay. The house had not been cleaned. Only the big construction debris had been shoveled out. Plaster dust still covered everything. Windows still had stickers on them. I looked at the Realtor and said, "You assured me this place would be cleaned."

"Well, they didn't have time. You needed to get in before the 1st and they were still finishing the house," he said. "There is a problem, though. The electric company refused to unseal the meter because of some little thing that needed changing. It has been taken care of, but they don't work on weekends, so you won't have heat or electricity until sometime Monday.

The gas heater won't turn on without electricity. I have brought over a gas floor heater that will heat the living room. Your gas range will work without electricity. I will loan you these two lanterns for light. The electric company has promised to get here as early Monday as possible."

Herb saw the look I gave that man. He had once told me, "Honey, you can say more with your eyes than most people can with their mouth." I felt his arm slip around me and tighten. Smiling at Mr. Stoll, he said to me, "It's okay, Honey. I have a few days off and I will help you clean this place up. At least we will be together." Mr. Stoll looked relieved and, excusing himself, he left quickly.

Paul and Herb put the icebox and ice-chest on the screened-in porch, off the kitchen. Everything else was unloaded into one end of the living room. We thanked Paul profusely and, as he drove away, he promised to visit us when we were settled.

It was after one p.m., and John was getting fussy. He was hungry and sleepy. Herb lit the water heater and started cleaning the kitchen. After sweeping up the floor, he cleaned the cupboards and washed off counters and the stove so we would at least be able to eat.

I fed John and laid him in his buggy with a bottle. The house was like a refrigerator, so I kept him in the living room with the hall, bath and bedroom doors closed. He was so tired, I knew he would sleep all afternoon.

We ate a quick lunch and then went into the hall with my broom and cleaning things. After shutting the door behind us, I rolled up a towel to cover the opening under the door. I didn't want our baby breathing that plaster dust.

While Johnny slept, we swept debris from the bedrooms into the hall and down to the living room door, wiped the dust from the doors, windows and window sills, and wet-mopped the floors. I then rolled the buggy into one of the clean bedrooms and placed the bath towel under that door while we swept everything into the living room and finished cleaning the hall and bath.

After scraping away the debris from the kitchen and bathroom floors, we had discovered that those floors were covered with a dark asphalt tile. The floors in the rest of the house were bare concrete, soooo cold! We had assumed the floors would have floor covering on them. It would be two years before we could save enough to buy tile and do that messy job of tiling the rest of the house.

I heard Johnny crying. He had awakened in a strange room and not in his crib. I rolled the buggy out into the living room where it was warmer. While I took care of John, Herb cleared a spot near the table and set up his playpen, found his toys and placed them in it. Taking his boy from me, he placed him in among the toys and stepped back smiling as he watched him choose which toy he wanted to play with. Still smiling, he said, "While you start dinner, I will go set up Johnny's crib. I think I will leave the bedroom doors open and maybe some heat will work its way back there."

Stepping out onto the porch, I searched through the ice chest for something for dinner. Herb would have leftover bean soup to-night. While it heated, I fed John his canned food, set him in his playpen and gave him a bottle. By the time we sat down to eat, it was dark and we had lit the lanterns.

I put Johnny to bed, pinned a blanket to the shoulders of his warm sleeper, and then pinned the corners to the sheet on either side so he couldn't kick the covers off.

Herb and I dusted off our bed, carried it, the box springs and mattress into our bedroom, and set the bed up. I found the boxes that contained the bedding and towels. After hanging the towels and washcloths in the bathroom, I took the bedding to our room and we made the bed together.

By this time, we were both worn out and so cold. That heater was almost useless, so we decided to give up, take warm baths, and go to bed.

Johnny was an early riser. You could set your clock by his wake-up and bed times, six in the morning and six at night. He always awakened happy and would sit playing in his bed until he heard us moving around. He would then let us know he was ready to eat. I heard him stirring and slipped out quietly, lit the oven, and left the oven door open to heat the kitchen. I found the box containing John's clothes and picked out a warm outfit for him. The tiny kitchen had warmed up. I moved the highchair near the door to the kitchen and went to get him out of bed.

Johnny was sitting up, playing with his teddy bear. His blanket was still pinned to his sleeper. I was greeted with a broad smile as his arms shot up and he said, "Up, Mommie, Up!"

I set him in his highchair and, after feeding him his cereal and fruit, I filled the kitchen sink with warm water and gave him a bath, dressed him warmly, and put him in his playpen with his toys while we ate.

We left the dishes on the table and together, with a damp cloth, wiped every box and moved them one by one into the room where they were to go. We carried the dresser into our room and Johnny's orange crate furniture into his. While I unpacked and stored Johnny's clothes in his dresser, Herb was working in our room, hanging our clothes in the closet and putting his things in the dresser. I would get to mine later. John was beginning to fuss.

I went out, changed him, warmed his bottle, handed it to him, and put him in his bed for his morning nap.

Herb folded the playpen and moved it into the hall against one wall, along with everything else from the living room except the couch and large chair; these we covered with old sheets to keep the dust out of them.

While I cleaned up the dishes, lined the cupboard shelves, unpacked and put away the kitchen things, Herb started cleaning the living-room floor, one end at a time. When the east end was clean, we moved the furniture over while he cleaned the west end. When he finished cleaning, he removed the sheets from the furniture and took them outside to shake out the dust.

Together we set the couch in place under a window on the east end, and the occasional chair across from it. The table was placed under a window near the kitchen on the west end. John was calling, so I left Herb to move things from the hall back into the living room.

After John had eaten, I placed him in his playpen and we ate. By dinnertime, everything had been put away and our end tables were back in use. Our next project would be cleaning windows.

Monday morning, December 30th, as promised, the electric company sent someone to connect the electricity, and we were happy to find that our heater worked well. The house warmed up quickly.

The wind had stopped and it was sunny and much warmer outside. While I finished putting the last things away, Herb used a razor blade to remove the stickers on the windows. When finished, he washed the outside while I washed the inside. There were only ten windows in that little house, so it went fast. We were done by noon.

"Herb, we haven't been out of this house for two days. Before Johnny goes down for his nap, why don't we take him for a walk and see what our neighborhood is like?" I asked.

Herb brought the buggy from the bedroom and I bundled up John and placed him in it. We walked in a square for about a mile, circling our neighborhood. We could see the beautiful, snow-capped, San Gorgonio Mountains hovering over the city to the north, and San Jacinto to the south. We passed beautiful little Sylvan Park as we neared Sunset Street, which marked the boundary between Beaumont and Banning, only four blocks north of us.

As we neared our new home at 2517 West Williams Street, we passed two unfinished homes north of ours. Hopefully, this meant we would eventually have neighbors with children for Johnny to play with.

By the time we reached home, Johnny was asleep and I carefully moved him from the buggy into his bed and returned to the living room. Herb was standing, looking through clean curtainless windows across our dirt yard to the street beyond. I joined him and we stood there together, our arms around each other.

Herb smiled and said, "It has been a rough twelve months since my discharge. There were times I wondered if I should give up school and get a job, but somehow you made the little money I brought home stretch like 'the loaves and the fishes.' Now, thanks to God, the GI Bill, Grandpa Arrick and your mother, we are standing in our own clean, warm home. Tomorrow night is New Year's Eve. We will be starting a new year in a new home, a new town and a new job. I believe our life is making a turn for the better."

EPILOGUE

When the War ended and we were discharged, we scattered across the country and tried to pick up our lives where we had left them, but we close friends never forgot each other.

Vi Bergman went back to Texas and met an army Veteran named Joe Bimler. He was a great guy, and they were married six months later. They adopted a son, Tim. We kept in touch by mail and visited each other's homes many times over the years.

Vern and Rose West stayed in their home in L.A. They came to see us in Upland, and we kept in touch by mail after we moved to Banning.

Kenny Hickel went back to school on the GI Bill and became a hospital administrator in northern California, where we visited him and met his wife, Barbara, and their children. They eventually returned to his home state and settled in Billings, Montana. We never lost touch with each other.

Austin Horn returned to his wife and family in Sulphur, Oklahoma, where he went back to work in his dry-cleaning business. We wrote back and forth, and on one of our cross-country trips, Herb and I stopped to visit and met his wife. Austin was the first of our gang to pass, but we continued to correspond with his wife.

Roy Nilmeier returned to his old job as Postmaster of Fresno, California. Herb and I were able to visit him and his wife, Gertrude, several times.

Floyd and Peg Hinman, with their daughter, Virginia, moved back to their home and his work in Montpelier, Vermont, and later to Marblehead, Massachusetts, where we visited and he took us sailing to Martha's Vineyard and treated us to lunch there. We were able to visit them several times on our trips to Baltimore.

Rita Kizis married Gus Mueller, and they settled in New York.

Joe Puccio went back to his home in Michigan, but we lost track of him.

Paul and Elenita White, the first real friends we made after leaving the Service, remained our very dear friends through the years. When our daughter, Danna Jo, was born in 1948, Paul brought Elenita up to Banning to take care of Johnny for the two weeks I was in the hospital. Paul took a teaching/coaching job in Tulare, California. While they lived there, the Korean War broke out and he was called back into active duty in the Air Force and sent to Iceland for a tour of duty. After returning, Paul taught in several schools, ending up at Upland High School. When Elenita's health failed, Paul gave up teaching and moved her to Hesperia in the high desert where the air was better, and he started a Christmas tree farm. Elenita is gone now, but I still keep in touch with Paul and we share our wonderful memories.

My brother, Wayne "Pinky" Anderson, married Mary Lou Krintz. He built their home on Lake Shafer in Monticello, Indiana, where they raised six children. He was White County Tax Assessor for many years. He and Herb became very close friends. Wayne passed away in 2006.

My husband, Herb Gunther, got his first teaching and coaching position at Banning High School.

After six years in Banning, Herb was offered a position as Principal, coach, and teacher at the high school at Twin Pines Ranch, a Riverside County school for delinquent boys, located thirteen miles up the San Jacinto Mountain, above Banning. This high school was under the supervision of the Riverside County Superintendent of Schools. It was a year-round job with 30 days off each year and much better pay. Herb had a great admiration for the Superintendent of the Ranch, Ralph Johnson, and the wonderful program for delinquent boys he had started there. Herb loved the program and working with those young boys; watching them grow and turn their lives around. Through his position at Twin Pines, Herb's reputation for having the ability to successfully work with troubled young men had been growing throughout the County.

After six years at Twin Pines, Herb was finding it more and more difficult working through the politics at the Office of the County Superintendent of Schools. After a particularly difficult meeting with the County Superintendent, Herb received a call from Bill Lacey, the Superintendent of Palo Verde Valley High School, in Blythe, California. Herb knew him, and when Bill told him of his problems at the high school and how he desperately needed Herb with his ability to work with difficult students, the offer had come at the right time. This was a much larger school with a lot of discipline problems and a weak high school administrator.

Herb walked in the door that evening and said, "What would you think about moving to Blythe?"

My response was, "Not much!"

Herb proceeded to tell me about the offer and his desire to accept it. He sold it to me by saying, "It is one thing to want a job and have to search for it. It is another thing to be chosen because you are needed for a job."

With many misgivings, I agreed, and we moved with our two children to Blythe, where Herb became Vice Principal of the Palo Verde Valley High School. Although Herb missed the boys at Twin Pines, we were never sorry for our decision to move to Blythe. We enjoyed the desert and made lifelong friends in that isolated but close-knit community.

After four years in the low desert, John became allergic to cottonseed and the doctor said we should get him to the coast. Herb accepted a position as Vice Principal of Earl Warren Junior High in Solana Beach, California. After six years, he became tired of administration and chose to go back to what he loved, the classroom. He was offered any position available and he chose to teach the mentally handicapped because, as Vice Principal, he had observed they were not being challenged and he felt they were capable of learning. He loved those neglected kids and they him. Within a short time, he was able to move large numbers of them into regular classes. He taught special education until he retired in 1979.

I followed Herb as he advanced. The first five years after leaving the Service were difficult financially. Our second child was born March 30, 1948, a daughter, Danna Jo. When the Korean War broke out, food prices doubled overnight. It became impossible to live on the pay Herb was receiving from the high school in Banning. I found a job in a drugstore where I managed my schedule so I had a sitter for John and Danna only a few hours a day. In 1952, Herb accepted the position at Twin Pines and our financial situation improved. While we lived in Banning, I was Girl Scout Leader for Danna's troop and President of the PTA.

In 1958, after we moved to Blythe, I took a part-time job as a Home Economist for the electric company. This job led to a better part-time job with the local radio station where I was invited to create and host a show for women, called "Meet the Mrs." It became a very popular interview program.

In 1962, after moving to the coast, with both children in high school, I went into Real Estate. Five years later, I became a Broker, bought the company, and changed the name to Gunther Realty.

After Herb retired, we traveled in our motor home all over the continental United States and Alaska, as well as western Canada and Mexico. I still live in the home that we shared overlooking the Pacific Ocean, near both of our children.

April 18th, 1994, just two months short of our 49th anniversary, my beloved Herb passed away, leaving a huge hole in my heart that I try to fill with beautiful memories, not only those of fear and hard times which I have done my best to share with you here, but of fun, laughter, camping, travel, and Herb's wonderful wit and sense of humor. Our love that began on a dance floor at Corona Naval Hospital never dimmed. We weathered the rough times together and celebrated the good, while our love grew stronger, truly a marriage made in Heaven.

I hope you enjoyed my book.
Please rate my books on Amazon.com.
Winona Ruth Gunther

Also by Winona Ruth Gunther, a memoir:

Papa Said is the story of a little girl, her three brothers and two sisters, who lived as pioneer children with their parents in the early 1920s on a self-sustaining 240-acre Indiana farm, a mile and a half from the closest store. This was the time of crank phones, kerosene lamps, and high-button shoes, when Model T's, horses and buggies, shared the unpaved country roads. There were no close neighbors or children to play with, but they had their babies, farm animals, and their dog, Shep. Their story is filled with excitement, humor, drama, tragedy, hope and faith.

Papa Said is published by Inspiring Voices. It may be purchased through your local bookstore or at Amazon.com.

Made in the USA
San Bernardino, CA
23 February 2017